HOTEL · ATOP NOB HILL · SAN FRANCISCO 94106

11/26/85 Tue

Dr. Kay R. Jamison
34 Beaufort Gardens
London S.W.3
England

Dearest K,

You are not on the screen this morning. I am still smiling about the lady with a movement disorder. That much activity on the screen would be very disruptive. If you could remain still, you could sit there, but you can not. It is of course the spontaneity and gaiety, together with the depth that are so important to my vision of you. You are a continuous celebration of life; defeat, even in your Dunkirks does not seem to be in your mental lexicon. I often wonder where disease melds into personality or the other way and never come up with a complete answer. I know I am not in love with a disease but, you are also very special; "... I have run faster, thought faster, loved faster than most I know."

I am lucky. If I had known how "fast" you are I would have been intimidated and probably not have probed so far. Thus while I am learning more and more about you I keep coming back to my initial impression at the Bel Aire of enormous gentleness. The passion may in time turn me to mush, and is extremely attractive. It is the capacity for understanding or accepting, however, that is most important. This acceptance is the amalgamating force that makes me love you. Total acceptance is what is allowing us to be one.

Love,

R

THE FAIRMONT HOTELS: DALLAS • DENVER • NEW ORLEANS • SAN FRANCISCO

For information or reservations at any Fairmont Hotel, call Toll Free 800-527-4727 (in Texas, call 800-492-6622)

ALSO BY KAY REDFIELD JAMISON

Touched with Fire:
Manic-Depressive Illness and the Artistic Temperament

An Unquiet Mind: A Memoir of Moods and Madness

Night Falls Fast: Understanding Suicide

Exuberance: The Passion for Life

TEXTBOOKS

Abnormal Psychology
(with Michael Goldstein and Bruce Baker)

Manic-Depressive Illness:
Bipolar Disorders and Recurrent Depression
(with Frederick Goodwin)

Nothing Was the Same

NOTHING WAS THE SAME

KAY REDFIELD JAMISON

ALFRED A. KNOPF · NEW YORK · 2009

THIS IS A BORZOI BOOK PUBLISHED BY ALFRED A. KNOPF

 Published in the United States by
Alfred A. Knopf, a division of Random House, Inc., New York,
and in Canada by Random House of Canada Limited, Toronto.

www.aaknopf.com

Knopf, Borzoi Books, and the colophon
are registered trademarks of Random House, Inc.

Owing to limitations of space, all acknowledgments for permission to reprint previously published material may be found at the end of the volume.

Frontispiece photograph by D. T. Jamison;
page 203: *Big Sur, California,* painting by Alain Moreau

Library of Congress Cataloging-in-Publication Data
Jamison Kay R.
Nothing was the same : a memoir /
by Kay Redfield Jamison. — 1st ed.
p. ; cm.
ISBN 978-0-307-26537-1
1. Jamison, Kay R. 2. Wyatt, Richard Jed, [date]—
Health. 3. Hodgkin's disease—Patients—United States—Biography.
4. Psychologists—United States—Biography.
5. Psychiatrists—United States—Biography. 6. Psychiatrists' spouses—United
States—Biography. I. Title.
[DNLM: 1. Jamison, Kay R. 2. Wyatt, Richard Jed, [date]
3. Neoplasms—psychology—United States—Personal Narratives. 4. Adaptation,
Psychological—United States—Personal
Narratives. 5. Attitude to Death—United States—Personal Narratives.
6. Grief—United States—Personal Narratives.
7. Psychiatry—United States—Personal Narratives.
8. Spouses—psychology—United States—Personal Narratives.
RC644.J36 2009
616.890092—dc22
[B] 2009011096
Manufactured in the United States of America
First Edition

In memory of my mother,
Mary Dell Temple Jamison

and for

Julian, Eliot, and Leslie Jamison,
Daniel Auerbach,
Thomas Traill,
and
The Snowflake Club

Richard Wyatt, M.D., 1939–2002

Richard Wyatt, M.D., 1939–2002

In memory of my mother,
Mary Dell Temple Jamison

and for

Julian, Eliot, and Leslie Jamison,
Daniel Auerbach,
Thomas Traill,
and
The Snowflake Club

The love you gave me wasn't fresh and young,
It didn't melt the sun or set the town aflame.
But it was warm and wise as any street,
Where hope and sorrow meet in bars without a name.
I only know that one day was a drink
And then the next was you and nothing was the same.

—STUART MACGREGOR

Contents

Nothing Was the Same

Prologue

When I was young, I thought that fearlessness and an easy way with love would see me to the other side of anything. Madness taught me otherwise. In the wake of my first insanity I assumed less and doubted more. My mind was suspect; there was no arguing with the new reality. I had to learn to live with a brain that demanded more coddling than I would have liked and, because of this, I avoided perturbance as best I could. Needwise, I avoided love.

I kept my mind on a short lead and my heart yet closer in; had I cared enough to look I doubt I would have recognized either of them. Before mania whipped through my brain I had been curious always to go to the far field, beyond what lay nearest by. After, I drew back from life and watered down my dreams. I retaught myself to think and to negotiate the world, and as the world measures things, I did well enough.

I was content in my life and found purpose in academic and clinical work. I wrote and taught, saw patients, and kept my struggles with manic-depressive illness to myself. I worked hard, driven to understand the illness from which I suffered. I settled in, I settled down, I settled. In a slow and fitful way, predictability insinuated itself into my life, and with it came a certain peace I was not aware had been missing. Grateful for this, and because I had no reason to know otherwise, I assumed that peace was provisional upon an absence of passion or anything that could forcibly disturb my senses. I avoided love.

This lasted for a while, although not perhaps as long as it seemed. Then I met a man who upended my cautious stance toward life. He did not believe, as I had for so long, that to control my mind I must first control my heart. He loved the woman he imagined I must have been before bowing to fear. He prodded my resistance with grace and undermined my wariness with laughter. He could say the unthinkable because he instinctively knew that his dry wit and gentle ways would win me over. They did. He was deft with my shifting moods and did not abuse our passion. He liked my fearlessness, and he brought it back as a gift to me. Far from finding the intensity of my nature disturbing, he gravitated toward it. He induced me to risk much by assuming a portion of the risk himself, and he persuaded me to write from my heart. He loved in me what I had forgotten was there.

We had nearly twenty years together. He was my husband, colleague, and friend; when he became ill and we knew he would die, he became my mentor in how to die with the grace by which he lived. What he could not teach me—no one could—was how to contend with the grief of losing him.

It has been said that grief is a kind of madness. I disagree. There is a sanity to grief, in its just proportion of emotion to cause, that madness does not have. Grief, given to all, is a generative and human thing. It provides a path, albeit a broken one, by which those who grieve can find their way. Still, it is grief's fugitive nature that one does not know at the start that such a path exists. I knew madness well, but I understood little of grief, and I was not always certain which was grief and which was madness. Grief, as it transpires, has its own territory.

PART ONE

Assured by Love

How like you to be kind,
Seeking to reassure.
And, yes, how like my mind
To make itself secure.

—THOM GUNN

The Pleasure of His Company

Death forces cold decisions. Five years ago, as I waited in my husband's hospital room the night before he died, I was numb with fear. The doctor in the intensive care unit had been blunt. "Mrs. Wyatt," he said, "we need to talk about what your husband would have wanted done." I reached out instinctively to my husband, the person who had made bearable so many painful things over the years, and for a short while was reassured by the warmth of his hand. The reassurance was illusory, however, as any reassurance must be when it comes from the dying. The doctor and I talked about what had to be done.

My husband, nothing if not a practical man, had detailed years earlier the final medical decisions he wished to be made on his behalf, sparing me now some measure of pain and uncertainty. Indeed, he had laid out with such precision the circumstances under which he wished to have life support measures removed that the attending physician cited his directives to the medical students and residents as a model of how such things should be drawn up. Dr. Wyatt, he told them, was a scientist as well as a doctor, and it showed in the precision of his orders.

Richard, I told myself, was also a teacher, and he would have been pleased to be teaching in death as he had in life. He would have laughed and said that, all things considered, he would have preferred to be alive and to have left this particular kind of teaching to someone else. The warmth of his hand may have been illusory, but the recollection of his wit was not. For a moment I felt the solace and pleasure of his company.

The decision to sign the papers to end Richard's life was difficult but peculiarly straightforward. His medical condition and the specifics of his advance directives made signing, however haunting, inevitable. It was a final and necessary act. More wrenching was the decision of where to spend the last night we would have together. There should have been no question at all. Every human instinct, every impulse of love and friendship, told me I should be with him at the end. It did not matter that he was unconscious and would not be conscious again. The desire to hold and console, to accompany, is ancient for cause: it is human; it is who we are. Left to my own ways, before Richard became a part of how I faced the world and my disquietude, I would have been by him all night, not willing or able to sleep. I could not have imagined otherwise. To spend our final night apart seemed monstrous.

Yet it was Richard's gift to me that I thought that

night as Richard would have thought, not as others would think or as I would once have thought. I thought of sleep, of practical things. You cannot afford to lose sleep, he had said to me so often, in so many places: You are staying up too late; you are pushing it. You will get manic. Take something. Get some sleep.

Medication, love, sleep: these were the things Richard had shown would keep my mind in check. His love would soon be gone, at least that form of his love that was physical and more obviously comprehensible. It was left to me to take care of myself, to attend to the practicalities that up to that point he had taken onto himself.

If I stayed with him in the hospital, a sleepless night would be followed by others in the difficult days to come; inevitably, the loss of sleep would push my brain over its edge. I might rail against such weakness, but it would do no good. I had been down that particular defiant and destructive path too many times to delude myself now. By all odds and within short order, I would become manic again. Having lost my heart, I would then lose my mind. Richard would be dead, I would be ill, a funeral still would need to be planned, and I still would have to live with the fact that he would be in the ground, cold and inaccessible. Everything—Richard, my sanity, my long-sought peace—would be gone. To realize a tolerable future, I had to turn away from the man who had made my future possible. It was expedient and an act of betrayal; it was rational in a way that Richard was; it was preserving.

I kissed Richard on his forehead, left him alone in a room filled with monitors that blinked numbers going in the wrong direction, and told the nurses how to reach me. Richard and I spent our last night as husband and wife apart, in cold and separate beds, an unthinkable distance from what we had known together for nearly twenty years. Richard was going to die the next day, and his quick mind and sheltering ways were going to die with him.

Richard was first and last a doctor and a scientist. Nothing else in his life carried matching weight. He loved science unreservedly from the time he was a young child until he died; no one could compete with the pleasure he found in grappling with questions provoked by nature or the human brain. I loved this about him. The same mind that served Richard well in science, along with a droll wit and a remarkable tolerance for diverse ways of going through life, made living with him a delight. Or, if not always a delight, certainly never dull. I cannot remember a time in the years we had together that I was bored. Nearly out the door on more than one occasion, certainly. But bored, never.

Early on, Richard wrote to me that he was new to love. He said this on many occasions and felt it to be an important part of who we were, a source of pleasure as well as vulnerability. At first I found this difficult to believe. He was forty-five and I was thirty-eight when we met; neither of us was new to life or to romantic entanglements. He was quietly but unquestionably charming, easy on the eyes, and confident in who he was. His reserve was seductive, as was his intelligence, and he was the kind of interested listener one waits for but seldom finds. He was catnip to women yet, savingly, largely oblivious to that fact.

We hit it off straightaway. We had many things in common—curiosity about the natural world, interest in the customs and love lives of our colleagues, and fascination with the ways the brain can veer off its tracks—and we made each other laugh. We were both optimists who bounded into our days with the belief that something interesting was certain to happen. We were inclined to find pleasure in whatever it was we were doing.

In time we came to realize that each of us also felt that we had been given a second chance at life: he by surviving Hodgkin's disease some ten years earlier, and me by having lived through mania, paralyzing depressions, and what should have been a lethal suicide attempt. We knew we had been saved by the grace of science and good doctors and we felt that we owed back because of this. We didn't assume that we had an endless shot at life, nor that life should be easy. Both of us had worked hard to get where we were, but we also had been lucky in opportunity and circumstance.

Richard, severely impaired by dyslexia, knew early on that he would have to work around difficulty. This first came home to him when he was in the second grade and he discovered that his class was divided into reading groups designated as "Eagles," "Hawks," "Owls," and "Robins." The Robins, it was clear, could scarcely put their books the right way up, and he was, most decidedly, a Robin. Not only a Robin, but at the bottom of the bottom of the Robins. He could read only with great difficulty and meager retention; his spelling was dreadful and his handwriting worse. He had, as he put it, the fine motor coordination of a clam.

Richard's attitude toward this was typical of how he approached problems throughout the rest of his life: he was philosophical and he worked harder. His stepfather, an antitrust lawyer in Chicago who had a passion for astronomy, encouraged him to learn about science and to visit the city's great science museums. These museums, perfectly suited to a mind more comfortable with ideas and images than words, became a second home to him. Neither he nor his stepfather equated his inability to read with a lack of intelligence, and Richard slowly worked his way through the science books in the local library.

Throughout college, medical school, internship, residency, and his scientific career, he had to add four or five extra hours of work to each day. He accepted this as a fact of life, grateful to be able to pursue his ambitions. I never heard him complain about the inordinate amount of time it took him to read or write scientific articles;

nor did he ever beg off reviewing the many manuscripts of the young scientists who trained in his laboratory. He felt he had had the advantage of inheriting a good mind and receiving an excellent education; he thought himself greatly fortunate in life. For the most part, he laughed about his frequent misspellings and misreadings and, once successful in his career, spent a considerable amount of time encouraging young people with similar difficulties to persevere.

Richard's combination of intellect and discipline paid off: he received his medical degree from Johns Hopkins, did his psychiatric residency at Harvard, and became Chief of Neuropsychiatry at the National Institute of Mental Health. Along the way he wrote or coauthored eight hundred scientific papers and six books. He was often asked, How dyslexic can you really be and write so much? He would laugh and say, Trust me, very. And he was. He struggled to write each sentence of each paper and had to reread, and then read again, medical and scientific articles. Each prescription he wrote he had to have read back to him by his patients in order to catch possible errors in dosage. Nothing, except ideas and enthusiasm, came easily to him.

Life to Richard was an adventure made up of worlds to be discovered and problems to be solved. The more intractable the problem, the more he dug in, mulled, tussled, and persevered, rotating the problem within his mind until a new way of looking at it emerged. He tackled with discipline and originality what my mind, given to restlessness and quick frustration, too easily skittered away from. His brain was constantly in motion, and little within its hailing distance was left unexamined. This curiosity and persistence paid off most clearly in medicine and science, where he made fundamental contributions to the understanding and treatment of schizophrenia and other diseases of the brain. He also found fulfillment in being a doctor to patients severely ill with schizophrenia. Although most of his practice was as a consultant, which meant he generally did not see his patients more than once or twice, he loved his clinical work and was painstakingly thorough in his diagnostic workups and recommendations for treatment. He and I saw many patients together, and I was struck by his gentleness and patience, as well as by how he encouraged them to ask him about things they did not understand or share with him fears that they might have.

When Richard received the first Margaret Byrd Rawson Award for dyslexic adults of exceptional professional achievement, he emphasized that he saw his learning problems as a disguised blessing. "I learned to fail and pick myself up at an early age, which is enormously practical," he said. "I know I am not like most of my competent colleagues, who can think linearly. I learn spirally, coming back to a topic from many directions over a long period of time. Because I must continuously relearn a subject, there is more opportunity to make associations that others might miss. Most important for me, learning is a long-term investment and requires a philosophy of life." Richard's victories in life were not at the quarter mile but at the mile and a half. He was in the race for however long it took. Once Richard decided a problem was worth his time and effort, he never gave up. Fortunately for me, I appear to have been that kind of problem.

Richard's curiosity and imperturbability made the task of loving me easier than it otherwise would have been. From the beginning, he kept close to him those things in me that he loved; toward my more disturbing qualities he kept, as best he could, an attitude of detached bemusement. He was able to do this well enough to keep us together, even when circumstances made it hard. A constitutional tendency to see the positive in people played an essential part as well. After our first Christmas, when I was living in London, he wrote to me about the challenges in our relationship, but presented them in an altogether wonderful context: "There are two Christmas presents that I will always remember," he said. "My electric train, circa 1946, and my trip to Kay via London—shall I compare Kay to an electric train? I shall. How fast could I run the train without its falling off the track? When it did fall off, it was picked up, placed back on the track, and ultimately the banking steepened. So I am with you." It took patience and skill to bank the slope, and Richard did it particularly well.

We were temperamentally different in critical respects—his passion for work over people; my intensity and less settled ways—but at the start of our life together it was my manic-depressive (bipolar) illness that created the greatest misunderstanding and discord. The disease took a serious toll on us before it eventually stabilized and, had it not been for Richard's light touch and formidable intellect, his adept way of dealing with the illness and with me, we would not have made it. Mental illness sabotages the best of relationships and, even in the most steadfast, generates an unrelenting bone-weariness. Early on, we found it hard.

Moods are contagious; they spread from those afflicted to those who are not. It is rare for even an experienced clinician to remain unaffected by a manic or depressed patient. For those who do not have the protective cloak of professional training, or who are personally involved, it is next to impossible to maintain equanimity. Moods are too insinuating, too persuasive: despair begets despair; suspicion and anger give rise to paranoia and rage. Concerned disengagement is the Holy Grail at such times, but obtaining and holding on to such a state is difficult; to remain impervious to provocation flies against all odds and is scarcely reasonable to expect from human nature.

In the early years of Richard's and my relationship my moods still lurched about. I was not manic or depressed in the same full-blown manner I had been when first treated for my illness—lithium saw to that—but now and again I would be swept up by a light mania, high-flying and captivating, which would then spend itself downward into a short but dangerous, often highly irritable period of depression. Brevity in itself buys no protection. Graham Greene observed that a Mediterranean storm may be over in a few hours, but while it lasts, it is savage enough to drown a shipful of men. Such is the ferocity of moods. I could live with my mercurial moods, but it was not clear that someone else could, or should.

Richard, new not only to love but to the day-to-day realities of the illness that came with that love, brought unique strengths to the situation. He was clinically and scientifically knowledgeable about manic depression, and well aware of its genetic basis; he was not inclined to attribute to character what he knew to be disease. He was curious by nature, in the habit of careful observation, and he possessed a charitable slant on odd behavior. He was able to make me laugh in the midst of truly awful situations, and he loved me in a way I never questioned.

Once, during a fierce argument about something that seemed consequential at the time but that I cannot remember now, I picked up a small, fine-porcelain rabbit, a gift from my aunt, and hurled it against a wall in our bedroom. The rabbit, which had gone by the name of Snowball, shattered into tiny pieces of white, unrecognizable except for the better part of one ear, flecked with pink, and a tiny paw. Out of the corner of my eye I saw Richard, who had a stunned look on his face. Then he smiled. Seeking to avoid provoking me further, he turned his back to me and struggled to little avail to keep from laughing. The harder he tried, the more impossible it was for him not to laugh; I could see his shoulders shaking. "Too much lithium," he said, after a long pause. "Your aim is off."

It was hopeless. I tried to keep from laughing for as long as I could, but, in the end, the two of us fell to the floor in fits of laughter. My rage was no match for Richard's wit. The next evening, when Richard came home from work, he gave me a small package; in it was a white ceramic rabbit, purchased at a local garden shop. Richard had written a note and tied it around the rabbit's neck: "In memory of Snowball," it read. "Who also went to pieces." "Snowflake," as we christened her, sits on my desk even now, unthrown.

Richard brought science, as well as humor, to bear on my problem with moods. He kept fastidious notes on everything he could measure: he rated and charted my moods against my serum lithium levels; my moods against my menstrual cycle; my moods and lithium levels against the seasons of the year; my thyroid lab values against the dosages of my lithium and thyroid medication. During one particularly turbulent period, he made morning and evening ratings of my moods and recorded them on a chart that eventually filled up with red and green and black dots. I clearly had become a project to him, one that was useful in figuring out patterns in my illness, as well as creating enough interest to keep his mind engaged. It built sufficient distance between him and my moods to help tame the beast.

On several occasions, Richard went with me to see my psychiatrist. He went to learn and, on occasion, to present his perspective on things; he did not go in order to second-guess my doctor's reasoning. He respected my psychiatrist's clinical acumen, and I never heard him suggest a change in medication or treatment plan. He did ask my doctor for suggestions on how best to handle my depression and agitation.

He took particularly seriously the importance of sleep in maintaining my mood stability. This was in part because he had studied and written extensively about the biology of sleep, but in larger part because he had observed firsthand what happened when I worked too late and slept too little. Mild mania had a way of feathering in, gently and imperceptibly, when I stayed up past midnight. Unless brought down by medication, which Richard first had to convince me to take, my high moods and proliferating enthusiasms quickly escalated into a serious clinical problem. Whenever I traveled to England or Scotland, or was many time zones away from home, I knew it was only a matter of time until Richard would call and ask me, "Are you asleep yet?" Nearly always wide awake, I would say, "Of course I'm asleep. You woke me up." He would laugh and say, "Go to sleep." Then, an hour or so later he would call again and we would make our way through a variation of the same conversation. It was nimbly done for the most part—neither badgering nor sharp-edged—and it made a critical difference in my getting better.

Yet, with all of this, he and I found my illness immensely difficult at times. For good cause, I had lived alone rather than have to deal with someone else's reactions to it. At times there was no facile way to handle the realities of my disease. One evening when we were talking in his study, Richard asked me about the symptoms of neuroleptic malignant syndrome, a rare but potentially lethal reaction to antipsychotic medications. I thought at first that he was bringing it up in the context of a book he was writing for general psychiatrists—it was a syndrome he had studied and written about—but there was something about his use of words, "Were you to experience this" rather than "When patients experience this," that put me on edge. Glancing around his office, I saw his black doctor's bag in the corner of the room, sitting on top of a file cabinet. It seemed odd, although I had never thought about it before. Why did he have his doctor's bag in his home study instead of at the office we rented together to see patients?

I asked him if I could see what he kept inside his bag. He was uncomfortable with the idea and only reluctantly took it down for me to open. There was not much inside—prescription pads, his stethoscope, a blood pressure cuff, a reflex hammer—but after rummaging around for a while, I found at the bottom of the bag what I think I knew I would find. Beneath the instruments of his practice lay a syringe and a vial of antipsychotic medication.

I didn't have to ask. It was for me, in case I became manic. Seeing the syringe triggered memories of being forcibly medicated after I first had become psychotic years earlier. I felt trapped and, more fundamentally, betrayed. Turning around, I saw Richard, who, like me, looked as though he had nowhere to run. He was a husband but also a doctor, and he had to handle, as best he could, an illness he thought was unlikely to recur but might. It was a dreary illness, and both of us had had our fill.

After a long silence, he spoke with an unnerving calm. "Kay," he said. "I don't know what to do." He was silent for a long while. "Medicine is imperfect." He paused again. "I am imperfect," he said. "You are imperfect." He looked tired and sad as he sat down at his desk. Neither of us said anything for a long time, caught in the cold realities of the choices we had. Then he added very quietly, "Love is imperfect." It was the most true, most chilling thing I had heard about dealing with the uncertainties of an illness such as mine. Richard was doing the best he could; we both were. Love was imperfect, but it was what we had.

Things changed radically for us, for me, that evening.

I had to take it on faith that Richard's intentions were good and his judgment sound. He never gave me lasting cause to think otherwise.

Over time, Richard and I discovered what it took for my mind to thrive and for madness to be kept at bay. It was hard-fought-for knowledge for both of us, imperfect and ferociously protected. My brain, as Richard explained it to himself and to me, was a delicate ecosystem, a pond of subtle alkalinities, which was kept alive through a finely honed mix of lithium and love and sleep, or, as he imagined it, "water grasses and dragonflies, and a snail or two to tidy up." Like Snoopy, whom he adored, he constantly rearranged his mental world, and mine, to make life more interesting.

From time to time, as the mood would take him, Richard would add new elements to my mental pond. Perhaps we should put in a koi someday, he said once, apropos of nothing, before we went to sleep. What did I think about adding a water bear, he asked on another occasion. Perhaps the koi and the water bear would hit it off, or perhaps the koi would eat the water bear. One didn't know. We would have to think about it. Sleep and medication, love and work—all in exquisite proportion—were the koi and dragonflies of my mind. Richard tended this pond with a blend of science and whimsy, and, for as long as he was alive, kept it hale and safe.

Richard's acceptance of me was deep, but it was not

entire. At times he was enraged when I was ill; at others, he was bewildered or coolly distant. He was not, however, fundamentally judgmental. He conceptualized my illness as unbidden, painful, and something I tried hard to master. He believed manic depression to be a complex interaction of disease and self and did not reduce its complexity beyond what was necessary to try to understand it.

"Diseases or disorders have their own character," he wrote to me after a particularly difficult time, "but they are present in a character. They do not take place outside of a being. Tuberculosis is only a bacterium unless it is in someone's lungs. Similarly, a person's character takes on the character of a disease. In your case things are even more complicated than with tuberculosis, because the disease is in your genes—thus you have never been without it and never will be. It is laced into you like a strand in a bowl of angel hair [pasta]. One does not fall in love with a gene but with all that is in the bowl, all that ever happened to it, and all that it affected."

He described in his letter the debilitating treatment he had undergone years earlier for Hodgkin's disease, an aggressive combination of radiation and chemotherapy that had cured him of his disease but at considerable cost. "We all long to be some whole we thought we were in the past, the self we were before becoming ill," he wrote. "The diseases and the magic bullets have left their traces or scars but they are not a part of me in the way yours are. All the more so because yours are integral to your personality. Because of this I am luckier than you; I can love a manic-depressive in a way you cannot love a Hodgkin's disease."

Richard's arms broke many falls for me. There were times, especially early on, when I would be hit by despair that had no good reason and gave no quarter and all hope would bleed out of me. "In the midst of seemingly unbelievable happiness with you, London, life, I find myself awful and dark and full of bleak thoughts and feelings," I wrote to him when I was living in England. "It came on as I suppose it always does, with a sense of tiredness, then the long deep clouds and finally just despair and Why again? What's the point? One's born just to die; feeling good is unreal and only to mock and haunt one when ill. And for a brief while I thought, I have Richard, and if he were here he would hold me and make love to me, make me a cup of tea, give me a pill to let me sleep through the hard rough part. There are moments when you provide a minute of sweetness and belief, and then the blackness comes again. I shall be done for one of these times. No matter what I do, this illness will always bring me to my knees. I accumulate sorrow and grief inside, which only wait until the next time to come out again, to remind me how always tides go out once in."

These times of reemergent depression were hard

when they came, but our life together was far from grim. On the contrary. I was well and in high spirits most of the years I knew Richard. We had more fun than we knew what to do with. We worked together, saw patients in consultation, and collaborated on many papers and professional projects. We each in our different ways had a chaotic mind and we found a calming quality in the company of each other.

Richard often told me that my acceptance of and love for him created a world of stillness and constancy he had never known. This, given my temperament, I found astonishing. I suggested one day that surely he was being ironic, but he said he wasn't. Perhaps, I asked, I was soothing only in comparison with his unfortunate marriage or other fraught relationships he had had? No, he said; there may be an element of truth in that, but not much. Possibly I acted as a stimulant does, in a paradoxical manner, to bring order to his desultory mind? No, he said, you create a quiet world for me. "Your stillness is a sanctuary," he once wrote to me. "The passion may in time turn me to mush and is extremely attractive. However, it is the capacity for understanding or accepting that is most important. This acceptance is the amalgamating force that makes me love you." It is strange, I think now, that love could soothe and draw together such different souls, and provide for them such hope, such happiness.

We complemented each other well. Richard was a reserved man, not someone who reached out emotionally to his colleagues as much as he and they would have liked. I think our relationship allowed him to know others in ways he had not, and once he got used to the idea, he liked it. "There is a loving of you that seems to ooze out to others," he wrote to me early in his thawing. "Putting my arm around a scientist in my laboratory yesterday—it was a natural unnatural act. [Maybe] it is just latent, having been there all along, waiting for the right stimulus to set it free." Although his first moves into a more emotional world were tentative—as he put it, "I find reaching out begins to dissipate with time and I start to revert to my regular tendencies of coolness"—he found that experiencing life more intensely was reward in its own right and that life could be found outside of a laboratory.

When it came down to it, Richard and I simply enjoyed being together. We had a number of close friends in whose company we delighted, and we went out several nights a week for pleasure or work or both. We both loved Washington, were hooked on politics, and when in a new city, headed instinctively to its zoo or its natural history and science museums. We were addicted to *ALF,* a television program about a small, furry, eight-stomached, orange alien from the Lower East Side of the planet Melmac who had crash-landed into the garage of a suburban middle-class family. We watched *ALF* avidly—to the detriment of work and showing up at Washington dinner parties—and were distressed when the series ended and ALF, captured by the American military, was unable to return to his home planet. So we spun away our hours coming up with alternative fates for him—medical school at Harvard (one of our colleagues there was legendary for conducting group therapy sessions with patients who believed they had been abducted by aliens), work as a war correspondent, a job as a translator at the United Nations—and drew up elaborate plans for his adopted family and his fellow Melmacians. Richard sketched out a complex new planet and galaxy for ALF, to which we added stars and constellations and cats, ALF's favorite food. Presumably we had more constructive things to be doing with our time, but it didn't matter. We laughed and drew and conjured, as though there were no end to time. Years later we were still adding mountain ranges and islands and inland seas and delectable new species of cats to ALF's planet.

Life was fun together. I remember a spring day in Los Angeles that began with dire wolves and ended with me on my hands and knees between the sheets of our bed, picking my way through a thicket of green and pink plastic "grass," hunting for jelly beans and yellow marshmallow chickens. Richard had transformed the bed into a "living Easter basket," which was filled not only with plastic grass and jelly beans but with all sizes and varieties of chocolate Easter eggs and rabbits as well.

It was a wonderful day, in the way that so many of

our days were. We started at the La Brea Tar Pits, which for forty thousand years had trapped and preserved saber-toothed tigers, dire wolves, and ground sloths. Four hundred or so of the dire wolf skulls were mounted on a wall of the museum built at the tar pits. Richard quickly drifted in their direction. He spent well over an hour captivated by the collection of skulls, calling me over to point out small differences in structure from wolf to wolf. I soon got bored—after the first three, the dire wolf skulls looked very much alike to me—and made my way over to the giant ground sloth. We were as happy as two people can be—in the presence of each other, but alone with our imaginings—and eager to share our mullings over lunch.

We had dinner that evening at a restaurant overlooking the Pacific Ocean, and Richard, after a glass of wine, took out two pieces of paper. "Write down the first thing that comes to your mind," he said. This sounded suspiciously like something a psychiatrist might say, and although he was one, it was the kind of free-association blather that was scarcely like him. He persevered, however, as he was wont to do once his mind was engaged in a new idea or plan. He handed me one of the pieces of paper. On the top, he had scrawled, "Richard." Under this he had put three categories, "Month of the Year," "Fish," and "Tree," each with a line drawn next to it.

"Write down what you think of when you think of me, and I'll do the same for you," he said. We started in on the list; once Richard had set out a game, it was futile to resist. We worked on our answers through another glass of wine and then looked up to compare notes.

"What month am I?" he asked.

"Early May," I said. "And me?"

"September," he replied unequivocally. "You are very September."

A little bit of wine went a long way with Richard. We carried on.

"What kind of fish am I?" he asked.

"A rainbow trout," I said.

He nodded in approval.

"And me?" I asked. I imagined an exotic reef fish, or a salmon fighting its way upstream.

"An anchovy," he said with a smirk.

"I hate anchovies," I replied. He knew this.

"Yes, but I love them." He smiled sweetly.

"It's not fair. I made you a rainbow trout."

He laughed and said, "But I *am* a rainbow trout."

And he was, of course.

Deciding on a tree was easy. He was a weeping cherry: graceful and gentle, complexly branched. I was an aspen, he said: tall, resilient, and "seasonally ablaze."

It all made great sense at the time, in the context of dinner and wine and laughter. And I think still, when I can think of it, that Richard was early May, a rainbow trout, and a weeping cherry.

Lilacs and a Roman Ring

Richard and I got married in the autumn of 1994, midway between our meeting and his dying. After a short but surpassingly happy honeymoon in Venice and Rome, we returned to Washington, Richard to his science and me to revising a book that was to be published in a year's time. The honeymoon, insofar as it signaled a time away from the concerns of the world, was over. The book I had written, an explicit account of my manic-depressive illness, guaranteed this.

Richard was unambiguous that I should write about my bipolar illness. Of course there would be consequences, he said. Some would be obvious and others would not. My disclosures would make me an easy target of criticism and would no doubt be of some embarrassment to him. The book might be a critical and financial failure. Still, he said, it was the right thing to do. People who suffered from mental illnesses, and their families, needed every voice they could get. As a scientist who studied schizophrenia, a long-time mental health advocate, and a doctor who treated severely ill patients, he knew, as much as anyone could, the need for public discussion. At a more personal level, he was the husband of someone with manic-depressive illness and had seen its damage firsthand. He also had seen how I and others had been hurt by discriminatory policies and shaken by unkind, if inadvertent, remarks made by our colleagues in private practice and in academic medicine.

He made it clear that he would do whatever was necessary to provide emotional and financial support. The former was critical, the latter not inconsequential. I had been financially independent since leaving high school and had worked my way through college and graduate school. Later I had worked absurdly long hours to pay off my student loans and medical bills, as well as to retire the colossal debts incurred during my free-spending days of mania. I was used to being independent. I did not want to rely upon Richard financially, but, given the alternative, I was grateful for his offer. He believed, and made me believe, that love would see us through, that we were doing the right thing and doing it together. I would not have written *An Unquiet Mind* without Richard's encouragement to tell the truth of my life. To the extent that others may have been helped by that, it is to him that a debt is owed.

The decision to write about my illness had been difficult. I am a clinical psychologist who holds licenses to practice in California and in the District of Columbia, and I had privileges at the Johns Hopkins Hospital. I am someone who studies and writes about the illness I have, and I knew that as a result of my disclosure my work would be subject to questions of objectivity by my colleagues. The deeply personal nature of my book would require that I give up my clinical practice, at least for the foreseeable future. The professional and financial consequences of doing this were substantial. I had spent long years in clinical training and had been treating patients for nearly two decades. I enjoyed broad clinical responsibilities when I was director of the UCLA Affective Disorders Clinic and had maintained active private practices, first in Los Angeles and then in Washington. Not seeing patients would be a loss, and a decision I knew I would regret. I loved clinical work and was reluctant to give it up.

I was as well a teacher of young doctors and graduate students and, like most people, had been brought up to be private about personal matters. My father, an Air Force officer and a pilot, kept to the military code that strength of character demanded silence and forbearance in the presence of difficulty. My mother, a warm woman, was similarly reserved in dealing with personal problems. Both assumed, as they assumed the presence of the air, the undeniable correctness of the WASP ethic that one kept one's problems to oneself, admitted no weakness. Being an Episcopalian didn't help. The Frozen Chosen had thawed over the years but still veered toward immoderate discretion. I kept my fears hidden and grew up sealed tightly as a vault. I did not confess, concede, or admit. It wasn't done.

I liked and believed in this view of the world. The people I most admired embodied these values: they complained rarely and got on with life. They didn't deposit their private struggles into the public domain. Their beliefs, which gave them an edge in assurance and ascendancy, made it difficult to acknowledge pain or personal failings. These matters were nonnegotiable and, in their certainty, they exacted a toll. But they were the only beliefs I knew.

Such values were suited for a simpler world than the one in which I found myself as a young woman contending with a sick mind. My innocence, which had decayed alongside my sanity, never quite came back. Experiences I had as an adult made scant sense in the context of my childhood ethic. I had been brought to my knees by madness and despair, my values shaken beyond easy restoration. I was a clinician and an academic, unavoidably aware of the devastation experienced by those with mental illnesses such as my own. I looked inward and then around me: it did not take much to grasp that privacy and reticence, however admirable, made life more difficult than it needed to be. Silence about mental illness bred a quiet ugliness and set in place the conditions for unnecessary suffering and death.

I found my own silence about manic-depressive illness increasingly intolerable. True, my parents had taught me to keep private matters private, but they also had taught me to think for myself and to have a sense of responsibility toward others. I felt myself a hypocrite, a repellent state that gradually wore down my instincts for professional self-preservation and concealment. I had studied and written about depression and bipolar illness for twenty years, had founded and directed a large clinic specializing in these diseases, and was a full professor at a major university teaching hospital. My illness had been under good control for many years. If I couldn't be public about it, it was scarcely reasonable to hope that others would.

I asked family, friends, and colleagues for advice. My mother and brother felt strongly that it was a bad idea to go public with my illness; they believed I had been through enough pain and that I would be personally and professionally vulnerable in unforeseen and damaging ways. My father, who himself has manic-depressive illness, encouraged me to write honestly about what I had been through. It was the courageous and right thing to do, he said, and I ought not to censor anything I wrote about him. Friends and colleagues were divided on the matter. Those not clinically trained were more inclined to think that openness was a good thing, in part because it might benefit others with mental illness and in part because they believed honesty to be intrinsically freeing. This was a far from universal view. Some were adamant that criticism was likely to be withering and the professional repercussions severe. Just as things had begun to settle in my life, they pointed out, I was risking additional instability. Those who were clinicians were even less sanguine about my being open about my illness. They, like I, had seen the prejudice and actions taken against colleagues in clinical fields; they had few illusions about tolerance within the profession.

I discussed the decision at length with my psychiatrist, Daniel Auerbach, a first-rate clinician who has been my doctor since my first psychotic break as a young assistant professor at UCLA. Together we weighed the potential damage of disclosure against its possible benefits. I was wary of being labeled by my academic and medical colleagues as a manic-depressive psychologist, rather than being seen as a psychologist who happened to have manic-depressive illness. I knew that for many the question of professional impairment would be a critical issue. This would be a completely legitimate concern. Those who specialized in psychology or psychiatry would present a special set of problems: I risked newly vigilant eyes observing my actions and appraising my moods, newly honed ears listening for skips in reason, real or imagined anger. It was an unattractive prospect.

My psychiatrist, who understood my desire to be direct about my illness, talked with me about the ramifications of openly discussing psychosis, suicide, and my initial reluctance to take medication. He, more than anyone, knew the cost to me of living in silence. But he also knew that once I had discussed my illness openly, my pride would take a sharp body blow. Pride had been a costly but sustaining force for me since childhood. Pride had kept me going when other things did not. I would be giving live ammunition to competitors, or to anyone I had irritated over the years.

His counsel was thoughtful, circumspect, and protective. It was without condescension. If I thought I could do it and had reasoned it through, he said, I could do it. He made the indisputable point that it would be hard, and it was. He did not say it would be insurmountably hard, and it wasn't.

I knew that my account of my illness and my life would have to be explicit, or there would be no point in writing it. This meant reliving, describing, and making public a troubled and contradictory life. I had hallucinated and been delusional on more than one occasion, been paralytic with depression for months on end. My behavior at times had been bizarre and disturbing. By anyone's standards, I had been severely ill. I had tried to kill myself and had nearly died from a massive overdose of lithium, the same medication I had written about in medical journals and strongly advocated that others take. In the early stages of my illness, I had taken it only fitfully and reluctantly. One could hope for understanding, but not assume it.

I spoke with the then chairman of my department at Johns Hopkins, Paul McHugh, in part because I respected his judgment and in part because I had to. I told him I hoped it might be helpful to others to write about my oddly intersecting worlds—those of researcher, clinician, teacher, and patient—but that I did not want to put the Department of Psychiatry or the Johns Hopkins Hospital in an awkward position. We both knew the inevitability of the "Who's in charge of the asylum?" quips. More substantively, there were very real legal, educational, and clinical issues. And no one could predict what the reaction of the public and the media would be.

My chairman listened carefully as I laid out my concerns. When I had finished, he looked at me thoughtfully and said, "You know, Kay, you have it completely backward." He mentioned the legendary surgeon William Halsted, who was the first chief of surgery at Hopkins. "It was known that Halsted was a cocaine and morphine addict," he said. "When he was impaired, his colleagues took it as their responsibility to protect Professor Halsted's patients. But they also looked after Professor Halsted as best they could, so that he could continue to do his research, write, and train young surgeons." He paused long enough for me to take this in. "If Hopkins can't do that for you," he said, "Hopkins has no business being in business."

He could not have been more understanding. He made it clear that I had his unequivocal support and that I should let him know if anyone on the faculty or the house staff made it difficult for me. He arranged for me to have lunch with the president of the Johns Hopkins Hospital, who likewise gave me his complete backing. He reiterated my chairman's statement that Hopkins should be at the forefront of lessening the stigma against those with psychiatric illnesses; he hoped my being open about my own illness would make it easier for doctors and other clinicians to seek out, receive, and give good medical care. Both he and my chairman were unambivalent in their message that they would back up my decision in whatever way they could.

They gave me the blessing of a great teaching hospital. I am not so naive as to think this is usual in medical schools and hospitals. I know that it is not. But it is exemplary. And it is from the exemplary, not from that which is done badly, that one learns and moves forward.

Inevitably, it was Richard whose advice and support were most important to me. He encouraged me to write my book, nudged me on when I balked, and took me into his arms when things were hard. He wasn't one to give up when life was difficult, and he did not give up on me.

I decided to disclose my mental illness in an article that was published in the spring of 1995 in the *Washington Post*; my memoir *An Unquiet Mind* came out that fall. Not long after the *Washington Post* story was published, Richard and I attended the annual meeting of the

American Psychiatric Association. Most of our colleagues, although shocked to learn that I had bipolar illness, were supportive of my decision to talk and write about it, and generous in their remarks. More than a few, however, seemed acutely uncomfortable. They averted their eyes, drew away, said nothing. I have never harbored the illusion that psychiatrists are uniquely compassionate or able to find the right words in awkward circumstances, yet I was struck by the silence. It was bone-chilling. There was a sense from some that I should be embarrassed by my revelations and, when I was not, that they were embarrassed for me.

That winter, after my book had been published, I went to a medical conference in Stockholm. One of my Danish colleagues said, "No Danish doctor would write what you wrote." It was not meant as a compliment. Walking back to my hotel, I saw cut tulips in a store window, scarlet and beautiful against the northern darkness, and felt again the loneliness I had known years ago as a young woman at scientific conferences. Meetings tended then to be very male in nature and were hallmarked by territorial rattlings and simian battles of dominance. To preserve myself against this, I often bought flowers for my hotel room: a splash of color, a trace of beauty, a private femininity.

Now, many years later in Stockholm, that sense of vulnerability, of exposed separateness, was back. I went to a flower shop and bought an armful of red tulips for my room and put them on my bedside table, an antidote to one male colleague's remark. Most of the Swedish, Danish, and Norwegian doctors at the conference had gone out of their way to be kind to me; they had been warm in their support. But one chance remark, not ill intended, threw me back in time, yanked me down.

For every coldness or drawing back by my colleagues, however, there have been far more acts of kindness and drawing in. At meetings in Dublin, my Irish colleagues were fabulous. The dean of St. Bartholomew's Hospital toasted me with a glass of champagne to congratulate me on my "personal courage," and colleagues from Trinity and University College Dublin were kind beyond reckoning. One of the consulting psychiatrists gave me a book of poems by Yeats, with a note that said simply, "Thank you." Another sent a breathtaking bouquet of tangerine poppies and wild cornflowers to my room. After dinner and an easy flow of wine, two other colleagues, professors of psychiatry in Dublin, took me to the General Post Office, heart of the 1916 Easter Uprising, and pointed to the statue of the dying Cúchulainn. We thought you might like to see this, they said, laughing. *He* had it really hard.

My private life was now exposed to all and sundry, and I found it hard to live with the new reality. As a child I had been quiet and invisible when troubled; as an adult, I had hidden my mental illness behind an elaborate construction of laughter and work and dissembling. Now, my mind and heart and their respective pathologies were brightly lit on a page, behind a lectern, on a television screen. Yet, despite this, it felt good to be honest, to be a part of the community I until recently had kept to the edges of. I was no longer just a researcher and a clinician answering questions about diagnosis and treatment; I could talk of my own madness and fears, feel not so distant, not so hypocritical.

I was overwhelmed by the many thousands of letters I received in response to the publication of *An Unquiet Mind.* Most were generous; many were disturbing. Religious diatribes were common. I received hundreds of letters from fundamentalist Christians berating me for turning my back on God and abandoning my Christian faith, which I had not been aware I had or had not done. Others thought my illness just deserts for not having truly accepted the Lord Jesus Christ into my heart, or for not having prayed often or sincerely enough. I had left my mind open to Satan, and he had entered in. Madness and despair were precisely what I deserved and would have in this world and in the next. I should expect to burn throughout eternity. I got more than a taste of the intolerance and hatred religious extremity harbors toward those with mental illness; it was unpleasant and frightening.

I was taken aback by the medieval quality of some of the beliefs held, modern incarnations of demons and possession, and by the viciousness of the attacks. One woman, who included a prayer card with excerpts from the Bible, wrote that it was a good thing I hadn't had children as I had at least "spared the world of one more crazy manic-depressive." There were several variations on this theme. "You are clearly unaware of the pain and suffering you and other manic-depressives cause," wrote one person. "How could you have even *considered* having children, bringing another psychotic into existence?"

There is a large and politically powerful contingent that is virulently opposed to the use of any kind of medication to treat psychiatric illnesses; they weighed in often and with frightening vehemence. Individuals who enjoyed their manias or regarded their ecstatic psychoses as a gift castigated me for colluding with the medical establishment by recommending medication. Others, a smaller group, felt I had written with too much affection about my manias.

Some people questioned whether my psychotic experiences were not in fact perfectly sane, simply visionary states or another, more enlightened form of consciousness. A trip I had taken to Saturn during one of my manic episodes and that I had described in my book seemed to me, when *compos mentis,* quite clearly psychotic. I soon found I was a piker when it came to intergalactic travel. Scores described their trips to Mars and Saturn and star clusters far beyond. Some regarded their planetary voyaging as a manifestation of illness, others as a useful extension of their usual mental lives. One person's madness is another's perceived gift.

Many wish to believe that the odd is not so odd, the bizarre not so bizarre, and there is little changing of minds once they are set. There are only so many ways to understand the strange and disordered. The Greeks imagined gods to explain what they themselves could not. It is human nature to invent reasons for why the mind shatters, hope plummets, or the will to live dies. Scientific explanations are complicated and, for many, less humanly satisfying than visionary or religious ones. They are also less interesting than explanations based on planetary misalignment, toxins, or childhoods gone awry. There is a disturbing gap between what scientists and doctors know about mental illness and what most people believe.

Some expressed resentment that I had had the advantage of financial security and supportive friends, colleagues, and family: What right did I have to complain? I could not possibly understand the real pain of mental illness. One colleague, hard-edged and drunk, in front of several of our junior colleagues, snapped that she thought because I had had a "privileged" upbringing, I had "no right" to write about the pain of bipolar illness; it was presumptuous. I found this outrageous. It seemed beyond the pale to have to explain to a professor of psychiatry that the pain of bipolar illness, like the pain of cancer, does not discriminate on the basis of "privilege."

At the end of the day, only Richard could make me feel less awful about the vitriol that came my way. Put the letters aside, he would say. Ignore the ugliness. If you *must* reread them, put them away for a week or so. He believed, from his own experience of having received stinging critiques on scientific papers, that criticism never seemed as bad on subsequent reading. Often he would call friends of ours and suggest that a group of us go out to dinner, knowing that warmth and laughter and shared tales of scathing reviews or wicked comments would lessen the hurt.

After a particularly difficult time, Richard planned a long weekend for us on the Eastern Shore, thinking that the Chesapeake Bay, which I had loved since childhood, might pull me out of my discouragement and gloom. He insisted that we do nothing but eat, sleep, walk, and make love. No talk of work or illness, no obsessing over the rightness or wrongness of decisions made. No dwelling on hostile letters.

I fell in love with Richard all over again that weekend and, as he knew I would, fell back in love with life. One afternoon, he went out for a drive and came back with a large cottonwood swan under each arm. Decoys, a male and a female, they had been carved by craftsmen on the Eastern Shore; they were beautiful. And, as Richard pointed out, swans mate for life.

Despite the occasional criticism and second-guessing, most people were kind in ways I could not have imagined. Acts of cruelty or criticism have been far outweighed by innumerable acts of warmth and generosity. For every discomfort about the loss of privacy or fear of personal or professional reprisal, there has been a countervailing relief in the honesty.

More than anything, I have been impressed by what people survive: the pain, the injustices of a health-care system that makes no pretense of fairness toward those with mental illness, financial ruin, violence, and most devastating, the suicide of a child, husband or wife, or parent. Everywhere I have gone, I have seen the wreckage left by mental illness and the resilience, inventiveness, and generosity of those who contend with it.

This mixture of devastation and bounty is most obvious in students who struggle with mental illness. I had been particularly eager to reach out to young people with my book, in part because the student years represent the age of greatest risk—the average age of onset of bipolar illness is eighteen or so—and in part because I, at that age, felt so alone with the uncertainty and terror of my own manic-depressive illness. For students who are depressed or who have other mental illnesses, the contrast between how they feel and the energy and high spirits they observe in their fellow students is razor-sharp.

Colleges and universities are incapable of handling the number of students with psychiatric disorders. Usually, administrative awareness of the problem is short-lived and ineffectual, stirred only by campus violence or the suicide of a student. Once the immediate crisis is past, there is little of a constructive nature put into place. On every campus at which I have spoken, students described to me not only the pain and the hopelessness they felt from their psychiatric illnesses, but also the lack of understanding they felt from their professors and college administrators; the lack of adequate health insurance; their fears about being asked to go on medical leave and not being allowed to return to campus; and how aware they are that their behavior is frightening and disruptive to their roommates (and the guilt they feel and are made to feel as a result of this). Always, I am struck by how far-reaching depression's presence is: a secretary or a department chairman; a football player; the university president or a trustee; a music student, a premed; a business student in suit and tie—anyone might be affected.

When I talk to students, so many of whom have tried to kill themselves, I usually ask them, Did you talk with your parents about this? Few say they have. They invariably ask me, Do you worry about getting sick again? How have you stayed well?, and I tell them, Yes, of course I worry. I worry every day. But it is good to worry. I tell them that it is hard to get well and that it is hard to stay well, but that it can be done. I find myself using Richard's words: Take your medication. Learn about your illness. Question your doctor. Watch your sleep. Use common sense about recreational drugs and alcohol. Reach out to others. I tell them that bipolar illness is a bad illness to get, but that now is a great time to get it. Science is moving fast, and public understanding is better than it has ever been; they are lucky to have been diagnosed and treated early.

I have been deeply touched by the courage of these students, struggling as they do to study and to compete, to love, and to stay alive. I admire how they have played the hard, unpredictable cards they have been dealt. They take less for granted and appreciate life more than do so many others of their age. I have enjoyed and learned from my time talking with these students over meals, in seminars, after lectures and before. There is a magic in being trusted with the stories of their lives, and if I had nothing but those days and evenings in their company, I would rest content and have little qualm about having made public my private nightmares and weaknesses.

Students have reached out to me and to their fellow students with generosity and ideas. Medical students at the University of California, San Francisco, for instance, who themselves suffer from depression or bipolar illness, set up a support group for other medical students and house staff with similar problems. To my great pleasure they named their group the Redfield Club and asked me to give a lecture in memory of a popular professor of anatomy who had taken his own life. After my talk, they presented me with a first-edition copy of Robert Lowell's *Life Studies*. It was a profoundly thoughtful gift and, by no coincidence, contained several poems I had used in teaching over the years. "My mind's not right," Lowell had written in one of them. "I hear my ill-spirit sob in each blood cell, / as if my hand were at its throat . . . / I myself am hell." I keep the book from the medical students on my desk, reminded of Lowell's hell and theirs. I am reminded even more of the good that some can seize from pain.

Most of my discussions have been with undergraduate, graduate, or medical students, but, because mood disorders often hit those much younger, I have spoken as well to hundreds of children and young adolescents with depression or bipolar illness. They experience the same pain and have the same fears as those who are older, but, because the illness is usually more severe in the very young, and because they cannot understand as much about their illness as those who are older, they have a particularly hard time of it.

One afternoon, I went to a high school in Northern Virginia to give the commencement address. The school, which specializes in teaching students with severe mental illness, had a graduating class of nine. The auditorium was ratty—a far cry from those in the elite private schools that hold such sway in the Washington area—and it was decorated with a decidedly nontraditional triumphal arc of black balloons. Each child had been to hell in his or her own way, and each had stayed in hell far longer than anyone should have to. Theirs was not a world of math tutors, lacrosse practice, and cello lessons. It was, instead, a world of pain, hospitals, psychosis, suicide attempts, and medication. It was also a world of grit, gallows humor, and little taken for granted. They were gutsy and admirable. The small band of graduating students marched to the stage to receive their diplomas, crosswise and out of step, to a scratchy tape recording of "Pomp and Circumstance." I can count on one hand the number of times I have had to fight hard to keep from crying in a public setting. This was one of them. Mental illness is pernicious in the young. Courage in the face of it is remarkable.

I was keenly aware of this when I talked with a group of children and adolescents in Colorado several years ago. They ranged in age from seven to seventeen and all suffered from bipolar illness. We talked about what it was like to struggle with depression and mania and to have to take medications with unpleasant side effects, how hard it was to concentrate and to study, and how it was nearly impossible to make friends and family understand. These were things they knew too well, too young. But we talked of hope, as well, and how one could live a good life with the illness. It was hard, but it could be done. I answered their questions as best I could. Then, as I was leaving, a young boy, perhaps seven or eight years old, came up to me and put his hand in mine. He looked up at me and asked, "Are you *really* okay?"

I put my arms around him and felt him sobbing against me. "Yes, I am," I said to him. "I really am. You will be, too." He looked doubtful. I reached into my handbag, pulled out my key chain, and removed the plastic Bugs Bunny charm I had carried for years. I told him it was my extra-lucky charm because it had not just one rabbit's foot, but four. A small smile appeared. I gave him the key fob and assured him that Bugs Bunny would bring him the same good luck he had brought me.

I hoped that this would be true, but the world and his illness being the way they are, I was not sure that luck would carry him as far as would be fair.

Six months after I first discussed my manic-depressive illness in public, Richard and I spent our wedding anniversary in Rome, where he was giving a medical talk and, as part of a bicentennial lecture series about John Keats, I was speaking at the American Academy in Rome. We had several days together of aimless wandering and evenings with friends and, on our anniversary, a romantic dinner on the rooftop of the Hotel Hassler, where we were staying. It was a sweet lull in the wheeling days that had become our lives. Late one afternoon, after a long walk by myself through the Borghese Gardens, I returned to our room, where Richard had been working on a paper. It was evident he had been up to something.

"I got you some flowers," he said.

I looked around the room and saw nothing.

"But first you have to find them."

His smile was broad, his mind afoot. I looked around the room again but still could see no flowers. The only place left was the bathroom, so I opened the door. Richard had outdone himself. The bathtub was filled with floating blossoms of white and pink and lavender. It was a stunningly beautiful sight. I looked at the flowers more closely; they looked suspiciously familiar.

They were. The day before, the staff of the Keats-Shelley House had kindly sent me a beautiful bouquet of roses and lilacs to thank me for my lecture. Richard, while I was out on my walk, had removed the flowers from the vase, cut their stems, and set them a-sail on the water. It was low-cost and very Richard.

He said eagerly, "Keep looking. You'll need to get down on your knees for this." Feeling mildly ridiculous, and wheezing because I'm allergic to roses, I got down on my hands and knees to explore the blossoms as they drifted in the bathtub. My hands were wet and cold and my knees soon sore, but I kept at it and finally discovered, attached by a paper clip and a rubber band to the stem of one of the roses, a pill bottle with a note inside: "Check the bed." It was a hunt. Richard was in his element.

After a prolonged search of our exceedingly large bed, I found a small red box. It was from a jeweler in Rome and inside, on silk, was an antique gold ring.

Underneath one of the pillows was a note. "Thank you for the happiest year of my life," Richard had scratched in his dyslexic hand. "I know that talking and writing about your illness has been hard. I am very proud of you—not only as your husband, but as your colleague."

The next morning, Richard dipped my new ring into the waters of the Trevi Fountain and then slipped it onto my finger, next to my wedding band. It would be with me when he could not, he said; it would lessen the hurt from the cool silences or sharp remarks that might come my way. After we returned to Washington and criticism did lay me low, Richard was wry and loyal and he brought me back again. When things went well, his joy was undiluted, and we hung the moon.

We laughed and made love through those Italian days, and thought our happiness imperishable. It was a time of such closeness that even now I cast into those memories for assurance. I had Richard, we had each other, and it was enough.

Time sped by without our believing that it could end. Love pushed back our fears that his or my illness might come back, that one of us might die. It was a blithe time, and it did not last.

PART TWO

Last Champagne

Medical etiquette called for a physician to call for two glasses of champagne and to drink them silently with his patient when that patient was a medical man who had just passed any hope of recovery. The meaning of the champagne was understood: the need of awkward words obviated.

—RICHARD DAVENPORT-HINES

Broken Portions

Richard was thirty-three years old when he was diagnosed with stage IVB Hodgkin's disease. This, in 1973, was a death sentence. A large tumor in his chest was growing rapidly; the cancer had already spread to his spleen, liver, and bones. Two vertebrae had disintegrated from the malignancy in his spine. There was nothing to be done, Richard said, except to read carefully through his life-insurance policies, write up the experiments he had been working on, and think of a way to say goodbye to his three-year-old daughter and his twin sons, born only months earlier.

Richard's colleagues insisted he fly out to the West Coast for a consultation with Henry Kaplan, the Stanford oncologist who had pioneered a radically aggressive treatment for Hodgkin's disease. Over the next two years, Richard received massive doses of radiation and chemotherapy, which saved his life. He attributed this stay of death to the fearlessness and the restless brilliance of his physician. Kaplan's "secular miracle," as

Richard put it, lost no wonder for him because it came from a doctor rather than an ancient faith or prayers. On the contrary, it intensified his childhood belief that science could do incomprehensible things.

Richard caught the morning side of a fast-breaking wave in medical science, and he remained indebted to clinical scientists, especially Henry Kaplan, for the rest of his life. He regarded the nearly thirty years of life he had after his diagnosis of Hodgkin's disease as a gift neither deserved nor undeserved, but an astonishing feat of medicine. He did not believe that the seeds of death left in him by the radiation were unjust. He knew what he owed to science, and he had an unassailable gratitude toward his doctors. Nothing changed those basic beliefs.

Richard stayed well for twenty years. The second ten of these were ours, a decade of health that lulled us into believing that his past medical problems were truly past, not the determinant of our future. The next decade, however, defined more by illness than by health, established that the arrangement between his life and his death was a darker one. Kaplan's treatment for Hodgkin's disease had been brilliant but imperfect, as science at its frontiers so often is. Radiation, which cured Richard of his first cancer, was to come back three times: twice nearly to kill him and the third time to succeed.

We knew such delayed damage was possible. Leukemias and other late-occurring cancers were not uncommon in patients treated with radiation; more recently, doctors had observed that a disturbing number of the Hodgkin's patients who had been treated with high-dose radiation were also dying of "silent" heart disease. Because Richard had been a part of the early Stanford clinical trials, our internist ordered a cardiac stress test; it had to be stopped. The year before we got married, Richard was treated at Johns Hopkins for a 99.9 percent blockage in his left anterior descending artery, a vessel subtly referred to by cardiologists as the "widow maker." Four hospitalizations later, Richard's heart was again hale and fit and, for a handful of years, he had an easy health. We were more wary than we had been before but thought, without thinking well, that we had paid our dues for his earlier survival of Hodgkin's.

It was never to be that easy. In the summer of 1999, fast and without warning, Richard got very sick. His weight plummeted and he found it hard to breathe. He no longer was the alert, intensely curious man I had fallen in love with; rather, he was dull and disinterested. I scarcely recognized him. Richard was fading away quickly, melting like the Wicked Witch, someone for whom, when he was well, Richard maintained a strong affection.

The scans ordered by our internist revealed tumors in Richard's liver, rectal wall, and lungs. No one tried to minimize this medical reality, although, in an unthinking moment of whistling past the graveyard, I mumbled something about the advances being made by our colleagues in oncology. This seemed improbable even as I said it. Richard looked at me incredulously: there was little hope against tumors strewn archipelago-like, so far and wide throughout his body. Richard and I were optimists by nature, but not insensate.

Neither of us slept that night, reaching out for each other, troubled and restless: talking, silent; lights on, lights off; looking through Richard's old medical textbooks—hopelessly out of date in their discussions of cancer—to find a phrase or a statistic that might dampen the horror for a while. We went through every "What if?" we could imagine—and we could imagine many—and then drew into our collective self, coiled around each other in some ancient mammalian way to fend off desperation.

The next day was better, in part because it was the day and not the night, and in part because it was not possible for it to be worse. Richard's preliminary biopsy results offered us some hope, as well; it was possible that Richard had lymphoma, not metastatic solid tumor disease. Lymphoma, in our new world of bad options, was a good thing; it carried the possibility of life. My Hopkins colleagues made an appointment for us to see an oncologist at Hopkins the next day. I will go to my death, as Richard did his, more than willing to walk on broken glass for him.

Richard Ambinder, the director of hematologic malignancies at Hopkins, took one look at Richard and said, "So. You look sick." This, in itself, would not have been enough to secure our trust; it was not a penetrating observation. The lucidity and rigor with which he laid out the diagnostic and treatment possibilities, however, and the insistent concern with which he regarded Richard's rapidly deteriorating condition, did catch our attention. Richard's MRI scans showed clearly malignant disease, he said, and it was progressing rapidly. If Richard did not get immediate and aggressive treatment, he would die. We had entered the blunt and exquisitely competent world of Ambinder and were relieved to have done so.

Ambinder said he would consult a Hopkins pathologist and one of his colleagues at the National Institutes of Health (NIH); if it turned out to be a solid tumor malignancy, he did not hold out much hope. If it was Burkitt's lymphoma, as he thought likely, Richard had a chance. Ambinder grasped Richard's shoulder and told him that he and the Hopkins staff would take good care of him. He then turned to me and assured me of the same. He took Richard up to the ward himself, talking with him all the while about their research interests and common experiences as medical students at Hopkins. I saw, for the first time in weeks, a trace of animation in Richard's eyes. I also saw him tap deeply into the trinitarian roots of his true faith: Medicine, Science, and Hopkins.

Ambinder told us that the pathologist would talk to me later that evening about his diagnostic impressions and suggestions for treatment. Things would get moving; everyone would do what could be done. No grass grew under Ambinder's feet.

The pathologist called that night. Richard almost certainly had Burkitt's lymphoma, he said, and he concurred with Ambinder that if Richard did not start chemotherapy straightaway he would die. His directness, together with his careful description of Richard's disease and its prognosis, made our decision relatively easy. He and Ambinder did not present an array of complex and competing options. There were no meaningful options besides chemotherapy, and there was no point in wasting time.

Ambinder had said that if Richard responded to the chemotherapy, he was likely to show a quick and dramatic improvement in his symptoms. This was true. I went to sleep in a chair next to Richard's bed that night and woke up in the morning to find him smiling at me, revived as from the dead. Not among the quick, perhaps, but a bracing distance from the dead. "I think I like this doctor," he said. "I think I like him very much."

A few weeks after Richard's dramatic response to chemotherapy, Ambinder recommended that he undergo a peripheral stem cell transplant. Stem cells would be recruited from his bone marrow into his bloodstream, removed, and stored. In order to destroy any remaining cancer cells, he would undergo eight days of very high-dose chemotherapy. His previously harvested stem cells would then be transplanted into him through his veins and stimulated to proliferate. In painstaking detail, Ambinder made it clear to us that Richard was a high-risk patient undergoing a high-risk procedure. Death was a distinct possibility. Death was becoming part of what we had to think about.

Richard was sick for a long time. He lost his hair, retched and vomited in places too many to mention, and became transiently psychotic from steroids. One day, as he put it, he shed his gut like a snake sheds its skin. Anticancer drugs were injected directly into his cerebrospinal fluid. He endured so many uncomfortable and harrowing procedures that what he went through was only partially imaginable to me. Yet he remained imperturbable and wryly engaged with life; he gave patience a good name.

Richard received a bone marrow transplant in early December of 1999, and then we did what cancer requires one to do: we waited. We waited for the results of blood tests and scans; we waited for the inevitable complications; and, most rackingly, we waited to see if his transplant would produce the cells he needed to stay alive. A normal white cell count is between four thousand and eleven thousand; at one point, Richard's was thirty. He was more tense during this time than I had ever seen him, keenly aware of the danger if his transplant failed.

Richard did what I had always known him to do when he was hurt or worried: he turned inward, to his imagination. One day, for diversion, he called up the names of all of the rivers he knew; on other days, it was stars and constellations, or viruses and bacteria. One night, during a particularly difficult time, he reconstructed in his mind, bone by bone, the skeleton of a dinosaur in Chicago's Field Museum, which he had visited as a child. As his physical health improved, his mind regained its elegant inventiveness. I came into his room one morning to find that he had spent much of the night conjuring up a brain nearly as large as his hospital room and had then set about exploring it. He hiked across its fissures and rappelled his way down the substantia nigra, a part of the brain he had studied and particularly liked. He swam in the brain's ventricles and bounced up and down on the optic nerve. Richard was on his way back.

Mostly he slept and I did needlepoint, or I read to him from Sherlock Holmes or from Antoine de Saint-Exupéry's *Wind, Sand and Stars.* When he was better, I read to him from Annie Dillard's *Pilgrim at Tinker Creek,* a book he had given to me shortly after we met. We talked at length about the naturalists and the scientists I was studying for a book I was writing about exuberance. He fell in love, as I had, with Wilson "Snowflake" Bentley and Bentley's world of snowflakes, and many times I came into his hospital room to find him asleep with

Bentley's book of snow crystal photographs open on his chest, or lying next to him on his bed.

Richard was discharged from the hospital on the winter solstice, profoundly weak and glad to see something other than hospital walls. We spent Christmas and its surrounding days in a Baltimore hotel near Hopkins so that he could receive intensive outpatient care. It was a difficult time—he was frail and his immune system more so—but we soon fell into a quiet rhythm that was not without its appeal. Each morning, we went together to the oncology clinic, where he had his blood drawn, and then we waited to hear the day's numbers, each of which took on its own significance and created its own anxieties when it was too high or too low. We talked to other cancer patients, which we loved doing and which gave us heart. In the afternoons, we went back to our room and listened to carols, or Richard slept and I read. We lay nestled together at night, taking joy in the season and in the warmth of our bodies next to each other.

Richard got better. He gained back his weight and we gained back our hopes. We worried less about each fleeting fever or day of fatigue and, after a long time's passing, we made love again. Slowly, gently, we fell back into life. One day several months after Richard's transplant, we went to Hopkins for a routine follow-up visit and waited for Ambinder to give us the results of Richard's most recent lab tests and scans. We had cause to be optimistic, but dread tends to trump optimism when one is waiting for results in an oncologist's office.

Ambinder lumbered into the room, radiant. This was a good sign; Ambinder is not an essentially radiant man. "So," he said to Richard, "I think you are well. I think you have beaten this thing." Richard and I, used to Ambinder's more usual bluntness and nuanced pessimism, sat silent and disbelieving. Then it sunk in.

Those minutes of pure joy will stay with me always: Richard smiling at me, me at him, both of us at Ambinder, and Ambinder at Richard and me. It had been a terrible, intimate journey with the best doctor we could have asked for. Ambinder had taken Richard through a grave illness and high-risk medical procedures. He had been blunt, clinically astute, and kind. He had not promised what he could not deliver. He had been everything one could wish for in a physician, and I felt toward him the kind of gratitude and respect you feel for someone who has saved the life of the person you most need and love. Richard, in turn, felt for him the kind of respect that, until that point, he had given only to Henry Kaplan at Stanford. Ambinder, he said, was a "doctor's doctor and a scientist's scientist." That was as good as it got for Richard.

We owed a great debt to the rest of the medical and nursing staff at Hopkins as well, and in a more abstract way, to Hopkins itself, a great teaching hospital. Richard was convinced that who he was as a physician, and much of how he did his science, came directly from his medical education at Hopkins. For my part, I had fallen in love with Hopkins the first day I joined the faculty and had stayed in love ever since. Our Hopkins bond was a strong one. Sometimes, after one or the other of us would return from giving a lecture or doing Grand Rounds at another hospital, we would compare our experiences there to those at Hopkins. Fairly or not, there was never any serious competition. We might acknowledge that another medical school did good science or had good doctors, but Richard would usually end up saying, with a trace of the romance that Hopkins often evokes, "I don't know. There's just *something* about Hopkins." It was a phrase we used many times as shorthand for how we felt: no long discussions, no elaborate comparisons. One of us would turn to the other and say, "I don't know. There's just *something* about Hopkins."

After our meeting with Ambinder, we decided we should do something to mark the moment. A believer might have suggested we stop at the hospital chapel, but Richard, who was Jewish, was not a believer. Instead, he said quietly, "Let's go to Hurd Hall." We sat together in the hospital's great clinical teaching amphitheater, where he and I had taught and been taught, and found ourselves absorbed in thought, each trying to comprehend what we had just been told. Neither of us said anything. There was just peace. Just quiet. Finally, Richard put his arm around me, looked around the amphitheater again, and said, "I love this place." Then we went home.

In the months to follow, we had our future back.

Richard threw himself into his science, we saw our friends often, and we arranged to give lectures without being concerned that we would have to cancel them. Richard worked on his studies of schizophrenia and started seeing patients again. I, with delight, got back to writing my book about exuberance; we began to make up for time lost and commitments broken. It was a magical interlude, gentle and love-filled, perfused with thankfulness. It might have lasted, but it didn't.

Six months after our celebratory meeting with Ambinder, Richard returned to Hopkins for a follow-up visit. Richard's most recent scans did not look good, said Ambinder. There was a mass in his lung, and it looked like cancer. The thoracic surgeon Ambinder had consulted did not think it was cancer, but neither of us found this reassuring. Unfortunately, we trusted Ambinder's clinical intuition. We would have to wait for more consults and the results of a lung biopsy.

We snapped back into the dark space we had occupied before with the Burkitt's, but tried to get on with our lives until we knew for certain whether Richard had lung cancer. We saw friends, we worked, we loved. But there was fear again, and dread. Uncertainty was in everything we did. For each time we did something of consequence, there was a moment of ice-cold fear, a question unasked: Is this the last time we will do this? How long do we have? How will he die? When? Where?

There was a possibility that Ambinder was wrong—

anything was possible—and this slim chance allowed us to make it through for a while. The last days of November slid into December, a time of year we both loved, and a time in Washington we particularly loved. We lived what we knew to live. My mother and I bought a Christmas tree and a juniper wreath and we strung the lights. We listened to carols and watched, as we did every year, *The Bishop's Wife.* We waited, with the rest of America, for the outcome of *Bush v. Gore* in the United States Supreme Court. We waited for the results of Richard's lung biopsy, which, when we got them in mid-December, were unequivocal. Richard had lung cancer, it had spread to both lungs, and it was inoperable.

Our initial reaction was paralysis, then shock. These feelings protected us for an hour or so, and then everything became a nightmare. I poured us each a scotch and we crawled into bed to talk and to hold each other. We were not by temperament inclined to view difficulties in our lives as unfair—we never questioned that we had been immensely lucky in friends and opportunities and in having each other—but this day was an exception. It was the first and the last time we ever said it, but it did seem unfair. We had just gotten back to our normal lives, or thought we had, after months of chemotherapy, a bone marrow transplant, and long months of terrible anxiety. We had spent our store of emotional energy on fighting his lymphoma and, once we knew he was cured, had put the experience behind us as well and as fast as we could. We had grown accustomed to having an open future again and to knowing our days as less worried, lighter and easier. We were beginning to take for granted making love again, and laughing without constraint. We had shed the greater part of our morbid irony.

It was a long night. I slept little and badly, constantly reaching out for Richard, burrowing my head in his shoulder, listening to him breathe. Richard, more practical than I, took a prodigious amount of diazepam and slept soundly. The next morning, we talked about what to do to make the best of things. Neither of us knew how long he would live—the life expectancy for his kind of lung cancer was six months—but we had always enjoyed each other's company, and we were determined not to allow the prospect of death to take that from us. Indeed, as we desperately sought some hint of a silver lining, we realized we would have more time in each other's company than we had ever had. This would be a good thing.

Somehow the morning and the afternoon passed; they must have. I built a fire in the fireplace, put on Christmas carols, and told Richard that I had planned a romantic evening—music, wine, and dinner in front of the fire—and that no matter what happened, I was, as always, his for the asking.

Richard began to cough, a deep and frightening cough. I panicked and immediately assumed the worst: we were going to have even less time than we had imagined. With a bitterness I did not know I had, I thought: Enough—God never opens a window that he doesn't close another two. My bitterness was premature. Richard pointed frantically at the fireplace, which was filling fast with smoke. Soon, the living room and finally the entire house were full of smoke. We were living an Addams Family nightmare. Squirrels, it seemed, had built a nest in our chimney, and while they broiled, we smoked.

Hacking, Richard and I made our way up to the top floor of the house, abandoning carols and romance as we went. I was disconsolate at what I had done, desperate that my plans for an evening of love had so ridiculously gone up in smoke. I couldn't even get the first evening right; what would happen in the months ahead?

Richard, seeing how I felt, put his arms around me.

"Thank you for the fire," he said.

He paused slightly.

"Did you know that smoke is a carcinogen?" he asked.

There was a moment of horrible silence. Then I saw the smile on his face, and we both burst out laughing. We were on our way to dealing with something unknown and awful but at least we were going to be in it together. And, we would have Richard's wit to help.

Richard's prognosis focused our thinking. I canceled as many of my lectures and academic commitments as I could in order to stay at home and look after him. We canceled professional trips to Davos and London and

Rome, but kept our plans to visit Los Angeles in a few weeks' time. We had close friends and family there and could read and relax. We could walk alongside the ocean. Richard was still alive, and we did not plan beyond that.

Certainly, the Christmas season was sad, but it was at times quite wonderful as well; we laughed even more often than we usually did, and reached out to each other with more need and a tender pleasure. It was Christmas made lovelier for our thinking it was our last. Life, strangely and redeemingly, went on in a rather normal way. Knowing that death was likely within the year, we laughed and loved and took little for granted.

A week or so before Christmas, we had dinner in Georgetown with close friends of ours, Bob and Mary Jane Gallo, both of whom had been unimaginably kind to us during the long months of Richard's chemotherapy and bone marrow transplant. Bob, a virologist and an AIDS researcher, was talking science with Richard when he stopped suddenly, looked directly at Richard, and said, "It's great. I can't believe how much better you look." My heart dropped fast and froze. It was only two days after the Hopkins pathologist had confirmed the diagnosis of lung cancer, and we were still trying to figure out how to tell our friends and colleagues.

Richard told them about the diagnosis. Bob looked stricken and was, for a while, uncharacteristically quiet. He and Richard were particularly close. Bob had been the head of a major laboratory at the National Cancer Institute (NCI), part of the National Institutes of Health in Bethesda, for decades; both were doctors. No one needed to say aloud what it meant to be diagnosed with inoperable lung cancer, particularly in the wake of a recent bone marrow transplant. I could see Bob taking it all in, and I could see Richard watching Bob taking it all in.

Bob shifted out of silence. He asked Richard to fax him the biopsy results as soon as we got home and to have the pathologist send him any viable cells obtained during the biopsy. He would consult with other scientists and oncologists to find out which experimental protocols might help. His own laboratory had recently synthesized a naturally occurring compound that promoted a form of cell death. He thought it might be possible to use this against proliferating cancer cells. To this end, he proposed growing cells from Richard's lungs in mice genetically engineered to have no immune system. (These mice were later christened "Little Richards," and, for a while, the tumors thrived as they should and died as they should. And then they didn't.) Bob said he would read up on Richard's particular type of lung cancer, talk with experimental vaccine and gene therapy specialists, and place calls to colleagues at the National Cancer Institute, Dana-Farber at Harvard, M. D. Anderson, and Sloan-Kettering. He would immediately consult with Richard's oncologist at Hopkins.

By evening's end, friendship, wine, and the possibility—the unlikely possibility—that science might outgambit Richard's cancer gave us enough hope to confront the immediate future. Our friends heartened us; our belief in science kept us from abject despair. It was the beginning of a quest that was to be marked by a thousand acts of kindness and capability from friends, colleagues, and strangers. It was a journey to save Richard, and it took place during an unnerving era in medical science. It was a time when, as now, hope could reasonably exist next to a prognosis of death; a time when the odds of staying alive or dying were whirling, inconstant things; a time when science could suggest, but not guarantee, breathtaking results.

Our difficulty would be to navigate between false and reasonable hope, and to avail ourselves of new knowledge that might save Richard's life while, at the same time, keeping close to our hearts the inescapable truth that Richard was likely to die. The truth would be what it would be; it would be what we would have to come to terms with, and it would demand our first commitment. We did not want to send ourselves on a fool's errand, flying after every new and as yet unproven treatment, but neither did we want to give up and cease to explore possibilities that might save or prolong his life.

When I look back on those darkly wonderful days of Christmas, I remember the gentleness and love we had for each other, and I can feel still the warmth we took in from friends and colleagues who reached out to us with such generosity. Dread would hit unawares at times, paralyzing us for a moment or an hour. But we found the dread to be as often as not reversible; love and friends, and our awareness of the shortness of the time that we had, worked well enough, often enough, to keep us from drowning. Richard ran his lab meetings from our living room and worked, as ever, into the early morning hours. I burned Christmas cookies, and broke my heart trimming our tree with ornaments we had gathered over the years. I hung the snowflakes made of gingerbread and the glass candy canes on the tree branches, and then added an ugly clay parrot we had gotten at a scientific meeting in Puerto Rico and a half-dozen handblown glass balls from our days together in London. Only the tinsel went onto the tree without my hanging a memory upon it.

Richard, as he did every year, put the angel on top of the tree. But this year, I had to help him. I felt him, so physically weak, tremble against me, and we looked at each other with alarm. Then we just held each other. Knowing that he was going to die, and knowing how little we knew about what was ahead of us, gave us an intimacy unlike anything we had known before.

We drove nearly every day through Rock Creek Park, a great and beautiful park less than a block from our house. We looked for deer, which Richard inevitably caught sight of first, and followed the creek as far as we could; we saved the life of a box turtle wandering on the parkway. We found places off the tangled capillary roads of the park that we did not know existed, and knew ourselves freshly beholden to the park's beauty for what it gave us now that we had not known we needed. A pleasure became a necessity.

We went one day to our old house in Georgetown, where we had lived for many years; we pulled up outside of it and sat in the car admiring the small pond we had built in the front yard. Building and stocking the pond had been a lesson in our differences, never more apparent than while debating what to do with the pond once the work on it had been completed. We had decided to buy water lilies. This entailed going to a water lily farm in Maryland, the kind of small adventure both of us loved. Neither of us knew anything about water lilies, so Richard described the size of our pond to the salesman, who, while polite, was less than impressed.

Richard said, "I think one plant will do."

"I agree," said the salesman. "Two would be more than you really need."

"She will want at least seven or eight," Richard said, nodding in my direction. "Why don't we take three?"

We drove back to Washington with our three water lily plants on my lap, talking about what we didn't know about water lilies. There was a silence for a while and then Richard said, "I trust you won't go overboard with the goldfish?"

"Of course not," I said indignantly. "I'll get only as many as makes sense for the pond." I looked at Richard, who looked deeply skeptical and then burst out laughing.

"Right," he said. "I can only imagine. We'll be feeding everything in the neighborhood that walks on four feet."

I made up in goldfish for what I thought we lacked in water lilies. At least a hundred came to join us. Before two summers passed, the water lilies had taken over the pond and were on the move over the pond's stone ledge. The fish flourished, despite the occasional electrical storm that left some of them fried and floating.

One evening, Richard brought a half-eaten goldfish into the kitchen and dangled it in front of my eyes. "Congratulations," he said. "We've created alfresco dining for the raccoons. They eat here, tell their friends, and then take one for the road." The fish continued to thrive, the raccoons continued to fish in our pond, and I never heard the end of it. Now, years later, I asked Richard if he remembered our trip to buy water lilies and the legions of goldfish I had gotten for the pond. He laughed out loud: How could I not? he said.

I think, until that moment—sitting in our car in front of our old house with its very small fish pond, watching the snow as it came down in great, beautiful flakes—I had not fully realized how wondrous laughter is, how fortunate we had been to have so much of it, so easily.

Christmas day was quiet and close. My mother was staying with us, and we had coffee and opened presents in front of the tree; the fireplace, now a source of mordant one-liners from Richard, had been cleaned and worked well. Richard gave me a pair of gold earrings from Newport, Rhode Island, with a note to wear them "in good times and in bad." In the months, and then the years, to follow, I did exactly that. They became a bellwether of my moods and expectations: an amulet to act against bad days, a glyph of hope or delight during good ones. We had dinners with friends, and drove around our neighborhood looking at lighted Christmas trees in window bays, their joy up against the dark. It was a good Christmas, all things considered.

We saw in the new year with a finger of whiskey, shortbread, and a shiver of dread.

Ambinder had turned over Richard's care to David Ettinger, a Hopkins specialist in lung cancer. He was to prove to be a very good doctor, open to the ideas of the scores of physicians and scientists we consulted from hospitals and laboratories across the country. Two of the scientists we consulted, Jim Watson of Cold Spring Harbor Laboratory and Bob Gallo, director of the Institute of Human Virology at the University of Maryland, had been friends of ours for many years. Jim contacted numerous scientists about their work, tracked down results from clinical trials that had not yet been published, invited me up to Cold Spring Harbor Laboratory to attend meetings on experimental cancer treatments, and introduced us to Judah Folkman at Harvard, whose treatment recommendations Richard and I believed prolonged Richard's life by many months.

Bob Gallo, in addition to talking with scores of oncologists, gene therapists, and vaccine researchers, continued to grow—and to try to kill—Richard's tumor cells in his own laboratory. He also introduced us to Jeff Schlom, a prominent cancer vaccine scientist at the National Cancer Institute, who together with his wife, Kathleen, was unbelievably helpful and kind to Richard and me; they became close friends, in a class by themselves.

The winter and spring of 2000 came and went and brought with them a generally quiet rhythm to our days. We spent our mornings and afternoons in the room across from our bedroom; it caught the best of the light coming into the house and became a room of our own, private and quiet and undisturbed. Richard worked on his laptop in a chair across from mine, and I read or wrote, did needlepoint, and watched the manuscript pages slowly accumulate for the book I was writing about exuberance—an odd topic, given what we were going through. Richard worked on scientific papers as well as on a short book, *Cancer Tales,* that he was writing about his experiences with lymphoma and lung cancer. In the evenings, we had dinner with friends or watched movies, or I would read and Richard would disappear into his study to work, often into the early hours of the morning.

Going to Hopkins for Richard's appointments with Ettinger usually shattered the calm of our daily world. We were anxious driving there, anxious while we waited, and anxious, if not distraught, once Ettinger had spoken to us. We spent a great deal of time at the hospital. While Richard was getting his bloodwork and scans done, I worked on a needlepoint tapestry of entwining tulips that I cannot, now, bear to look at. Our time in the "infusion" room, where Richard received his chemotherapy, was better, and after a while, it did not seem so alien: Richard listened to Harry Potter books on tape and I read or did my needlework, we held hands, or we talked with other patients and their families.

Life unfolded, as it will. Richard continued to feel reasonably well during the spring of 2001, although his scans showed slow growth of the tumors in his lungs. At some point, it became clear that the chemotherapy was having no effect, so we pursued experimental treatment options. We spoke to a vaccine expert at Georgetown University, who said that Richard, because of his recent bone marrow transplant, was not eligible for the vaccine trial. If necessary, however, he said he would apply to the National Cancer Institute for a compassionate use waiver. The NCI research protocols made it absurdly difficult for Richard to participate, however: Could he give *truly* informed consent? This seemed to us to be on the other side of *Alice in Wonderland;* Richard was a physician and a scientist, he had a terminal illness, and he had conducted clinical studies for thirty years at the National Institutes of Health. If he couldn't give informed consent, who could?

Fortunately, our friend Jeff Schlom, who is chief of the tumor immunology lab at the NCI, offered to help Richard with the inordinately complicated application procedure. In the meantime, Richard and Ettinger consulted with Judah Folkman and decided to try his treatment protocol, which was designed to limit the growth of the blood supply to tumors. There were, we were discovering, many options on the cusp of viability. Richard noted wryly that he loved being on the cutting edge of science, even if he turned out to be that edge.

Richard went through the standard treatments for lung cancer and then the experimental ones. He lived a year longer than had been predicted for his type of disease, a year that was a gift of science and the hard work of people who did everything they could to save Richard's life. But the tumors in his lungs grew; they grew erratically, sometimes not for weeks or months, but they grew.

Science and medicine cannot be pushed beyond a certain point. Richard lived longer than initially expected because of the remarkable scientific times in which we live. He died because there are limits to knowledge. We knew these limits well—we saw them every day in studying and treating schizophrenia and depressive illnesses—and we were generally philosophical about them, Richard more so than I. Both of us, in our clinical teaching, had often quoted Sir William Osler, the first physician in chief at Johns Hopkins. "In seeking absolute truth we aim at the unattainable," Osler had said, but we must be content with "broken portions." I wanted the unattainable. I wanted Richard to live. I understood the concept of broken portions, but I wasn't resigned to it.

The first daffodils came. We drove to the Tidal Basin early in the mornings and took in the cherry blossoms and, on occasion, drove to Theodore Roosevelt Island. Life was often normal, although in some ways more wonderful, as we knew that it was not at all normal. We continued our long drives through Rock Creek Park, usually taking Pumpkin, our basset hound, along and listening to the songs of Stephen Foster and Paul Robeson. These were small, shared passions—the park, the beauty of Washington, Foster and Robeson—and they gave a sustaining happiness to our days.

That spring, Richard was honored by his colleagues on three different occasions, and each was a source of great pleasure for him. Although the tributes were triggered by his likely death, he did not find them melancholic events. On the contrary, he could not have enjoyed them more. The first, a scientific meeting on schizophrenia, was dedicated to him by the psychiatrists working in Veterans Administration hospitals across the country. In their remarks, his colleagues described him as a "towering" figure in psychiatry, science, and medicine. He reveled in the "towering."

To a person, they acknowledged him for his pioneering contributions to understanding the brain and schizophrenia, for improving the treatment of schizophrenia and other psychotic illnesses, and for his generosity as a teacher of young doctors and scientists. At a dinner in his honor, the director of the National Institute of Mental Health, now provost at Harvard, talked about Richard's groundbreaking work in psychiatry. Then he said, to great laughter, that Richard's good papers had been published in *Science,* his rejects in *Nature.* Richard loved every minute of the conference, as he loved an equally generous and warm day of tributes from his colleagues at Columbia University in New York, where he held a faculty appointment and had collaborated with many of the physicians and scientists.

The National Institutes of Health paid him the unusual tribute of hosting an all-day scientific symposium in his honor, followed by a dinner at the Army-Navy Club. Many of the world's most distinguished neuroscientists talked about Richard's influence on their work. They talked, as well, about his grace and formidable energy, his generosity as a mentor, and his scientific creativity. Richard was deeply moved by these tributes. I rarely saw him cry during the years I knew him, but at one point during the remarks I saw tears that he could not hold back. Respect from one's peers is not for sale, and Richard, of all people, knew this.

Richard wrote in *Cancer Tales* that those days of recognition from his colleagues helped him get through his illness and face the prospect of death. He knew that he was loved; he knew he had made a difference. He believed that everyone has an obligation to give back in life, particularly those who have had advantages. Listening to the heartfelt appreciation of so many of the scientists he had trained or worked with made him believe that he had given back as best he could. He did not write or talk much about death, but during this time of tributes he did:

> Many people think about death every day. Call me shallow—many have—but it is a rare day when I concern myself with my own death. Long ago, I decided that if I paid my debts I would not worry about death. As I was growing up, it occurred to me that I had been very fortunate—I had been given a great deal and owed a large debt. I had been healthy, born and raised in the United States, was well-educated, privileged to go to medical school and finish my training. By the time I was

> thirty-three years old and developed Hodgkin's disease, I believed I had performed a sufficient number of good deeds that I had paid back my debts—I might even be even. Being successfully treated for Hodgkin's left me in the hole again. So I spent the next few years getting myself on the right side of the ledger. Certainly there were many times I did things that hurt others or committed sins of omission, but by my accounting I stayed ahead and feel I am still ahead. For me, not being in debt means I do not have to be concerned about death.

Richard's views on death were not my own—death to me is unimaginable and horrifying—but he gave me an enviable slant on it.

Raining Stars

Richard and I were given a long Indian summer before he died, a year beyond what we had banked on. After the round of tributes from his colleagues, Richard suggested a vacation in California. We had no talks to give or schedule to keep; we could relax, spend time with family and friends, and enjoy what we had. We could worry later about what was to come. It was a perfect interlude. Richard, who was still in reasonable health, sat on the deck of our family house in Pacific Palisades and worked on his laptop, or slept in the sun. In the mornings, I walked to the bluffs overlooking the Pacific or down to the ocean; in the afternoons I sat on the deck next to Richard and read.

Everywhere there were the defining scents and colors of Southern California: sweet jasmine, pungent eucalyptus; bougainvillea vines with their hooked thorns and papery blossoms of tangerine and fuchsia. The jarring blue hibiscus. Richard particularly loved the camphor trees, as I did the eucalyptus, so we drove the streets of

the Palisades with the car windows open, inhaling and happy. On one of our daily drives, Richard mentioned that camphor had been used centuries earlier to treat mania. He insisted we stop to gather some leaves: "Just in case," he said with a smile. I told him that camphor sounded better to me than an injection of the antipsychotic he carried in his black bag, so I gathered up an armful of glossy leaves. We put these in a basket to ward off madness and, as he pointed out, from that point onward not only madness, but also moths kept their distance. We saw friends and family, visited with colleagues at UCLA, and at night drove up the twisting streets into the hills behind our house and looked out on the lights of Los Angeles and the unfurling of moonlight over Santa Monica Bay. We made time stop for a while, and knew how lucky we were.

I fashioned a peace with California during that trip with Richard, one that was long past due. Los Angeles had always nettled me: I loved it, I disavowed it, I tried to put it behind me. I came of age in Los Angeles and, in that sense, it would always be my city: I first knew desire there, and madness; first made love and fell in love. Los Angeles was my original city of passion and disappointment: it was where my mind cracked and where, twenty years after the fact, I still felt a cringing shame for things I had said or done when manic. But it was also where I had first heard Schumann's piano works and Beethoven's *Missa Solemnis*; had, on a summer day, watched the first moon landing; first read Yeats and Lowell and Darwin. Nothing about Los Angeles was straightforward to me.

Great chunks of my life—great frightening, marvelous chunks of my life—were tangled in the passing of Southern California's strange nonseasons. Washington would be my first home and my last, but California was the fitful, bewildering center. Only Big Sur remained uncomplicated to me. I loved it without reservation, and sought it out time and again because it was wild and beautiful, and because it could settle me in ways that no other place or person could. Even when I went mad in Big Sur, it was an ecstatic madness, an astonishingly beautiful voyage of my mind to Saturn and its rings and moons, and to distant stars. I walked off my unrest along the seacoast of the Big Sur: away, alone, and unbeholden. It was where I went for desolate beauty and for the belief that here, always, I would be at home. Southern California I kept at bay.

Now, with Richard gravely ill, my fractiousness with California seemed a waste of time and energy, not to say indulgent. Richard was dying, it was our last trip together to California, and nothing else was important. I had wasted enough of my life thinking about despair and insanity. It was not California that was wanting, it was me. Robert Frost wrote that when those who withhold themselves from the land yield to it, they find salvation in the surrender. This was true for me. I took a different view of the West Coast, more generous and circumspect; old discontents slipped away.

Richard did not need to surrender. He did not take on unnecessary battles in life, and this gave to him a strength in character I did not have. We loved our long days in California; we took them in and kept them close, wrapped our life in the June sun and the odd scents and surreal colors of the land around us. Richard had a way of giving back to me important things I had lost along the way.

One afternoon he and I sat on a bench overlooking the Pacific, lizardlike in the sun, talking about not much of anything important, only small and binding things. After a while he said, in an even voice, "We should talk about the funeral." I tried to keep my voice steady, which was impossible.

"Yes, of course," I said.

Richard's suggestion was not entirely out of the blue, although in the sun and the quiet it felt that way. Earlier in the day, we had been to see Clarke Oler, an Episcopal priest who had been the rector of my church when I lived in Los Angeles. I had known and been close to Clarke for twenty-five years, and Richard was particularly fond of him. He had officiated at the religious service for our marriage at St. Alban's Episcopal Church in Westwood, held some time after our civil ceremony in the Shenandoah Valley. We had turned to him to talk about the things we would have to do in the months to come. We talked specifically, at Richard's request, about possible music and readings for his funeral. Later, as Richard and I sat on the bench overlooking the ocean, on an impossibly beautiful day, we continued our discussion of hymns and pallbearers and the ancient rites of final passage. No amount of God's sun could take the chill from what we were doing.

We went as far as we could and then, thankfully, Richard said, "Enough of this. Let's go shop for your birthday." He suggested a store on San Vincente Boulevard we had been to before and, once there, asked to speak with the jewelry designer. "She likes moonstones and aquamarines," he told her. "She's a bit like them: moody and lovely. More moonstone than aquamarine." He smiled his wonderful smile and caught the designer in his net of charm. And me, as always, all over again. He then traced out the design of the bracelet he wanted for me, one he must have been planning for a while. It was to be alternating cabochon aquamarines and moonstones, strung together by delicate links of gold. He wanted the aquamarines to be oval and the moonstones round; it was to be one of a kind.

The bracelet arrived in Washington several weeks later, a strikingly beautiful strand of mutable gray and pale blue stones. It was indeed moody, and it was stunning. Richard tried to fasten the bracelet on my wrist but could not; the clasp was too fine and his hand shook too much. So we christened it instead, continuing

Richard's tradition of dipping newly gotten jewelry in Italian fountains, gin fizzes, or the North Sea. This time he dipped it in a shot of Dalwhinnie, a single-malt whiskey we were partial to. "For us," he said, christening the bracelet. "For you. For love." I could not put the bracelet on then, or ever, without the help of someone else. It was an elegant string of stones, brought into existence by love, but it was not easy to wear. It was our life.

Our last summer was a good one. We returned from Los Angeles to find our garden lit up with a wild proliferation of fireflies at night and the Washington skies lit up with summer thunderstorms reminiscent of the *Dies Irae* from Verdi's *Requiem.* Richard was able to eat steak and corn and peach cobbler, which gave us the illusion of greater health than he had, and we had long evenings of laughter and friendship. Those summer nights with our friends were the moon and the stars to both of us; they will be with me until I cease to remember anything. Our conversations leapt everywhere: from the misbegotten love affairs of our colleagues to scandals in science, from stem cell research to Thomas Aquinas. We talked about the elegance of the universe and how we thought the world would end. We talked on and on through the summer nights, taking in more wine than others would have said was good for us, and spoke of Rome and politics, of our families, and of sundry microbes, any of which would cause a thinking person to pray for a competence the government did not possess. These evenings of friendship were unrivaled times, tinged by the overhanging apprehension of Richard's mortality. It was fierce and gentle friendship, and it made our way to his death more navigable, less lonely.

There was a fine-tuning of Richard's and my temperaments during the years we lived with his heart disease, lymphoma, and lung cancer. Before, our differences had triggered sporadic tension; now our basic natures served us better. Our sensibilities and quirks evolved into something more shared and complex, more mingled. The intensity of my moods and periodic flares ebbed with time and with the seriousness of circumstance. Richard's reserved ways changed into something more intense, outward, and nuanced. He became more responsive to the feelings of others, and held his emotions less close to his chest. He had always been physically affectionate with me, but now he sought me even more. When I came into a room, after even a short absence, he held on to me in a way I had not known him to do before. Just to feel. To sense. To draw upon.

Later, when he no longer had the strength to take a bath, he reached out to take in the world beyond him in newer ways. He would ask, after I had bathed, to breathe in the scents on my arms and my neck, to take in the smell of the honeysuckle or moss rose, lime blossom salts or eucalyptus. He had never done this before, and indeed had laughed at my many bottles and jars. Kay's

Excess of Scents, he would say to our friends: Why have one bottle when you can have seven?

Richard kept his essential privacy; he had been and would remain a private man. But he reached out more to other people. Acquaintances and colleagues saw the warmer side of him that I and a few others had always known. And now, when he reached out for me, vulnerable, I was glad that I could bring to him a calmer self. I was someone he could put his faith in, and it gave me pleasure. For so long, for so many years, I had needed him, leaned upon his love and judgment. Through him, I had rediscovered some semblance of my true North, and now he drew upon his gift to me. There was fairness in all of this.

The summer drew to a close in quiet ways. Richard felt well enough to work hard on his science and to see patients. I wrote and worked at Hopkins and looked after him. The tumor in his right lung grew.

In early September, the Pentagon and the World Trade Center were attacked. I was on an early-morning flight to Atlanta for meetings at the Carter Center; it took off forty minutes before the first hijacked airplane flew into the World Trade Center and landed twenty minutes after American Airlines Flight 77 had crashed into the west side of the Pentagon. By the time I arrived at the Carter Center, it was ringed by Secret Service cars dispatched to protect President and Mrs. Carter.

The telephone lines to Washington were choked, and

it was late in the day before I could reach Richard. When at last we were able to talk, he described the eerie sight of hundreds of Washingtonians walking as fast as they could up Connecticut Avenue, briefcases in hand, talking into their cell phones and looking unmoored. I felt panicked at being so far away from him and from Washington, but I could not get back. No planes were flying, buses and trains along the eastern seaboard were moribund, and all rental cars and trucks had been taken within hours of Atlanta's airport having been shut down. My only option was to rent a limousine, but even that would not be possible for two days. So I settled into obsessively watching CNN and trying to keep in touch with Richard.

The evening after the attacks, a few of us had a quiet dinner with President and Mrs. Carter. They were calm, philosophical, and tough. They spoke from their unique perspective on America about its strengths: the vastness of its lands, the inventiveness and resilience of its people. The weeks to come were to be shot through with the kind of straightforward patriotism they embodied that evening, a good and necessary thing. It was not yet the time for overdone and alienating nationalism.

The trip from Atlanta to Washington was unnerving. Flags were at half-mast everywhere, from Georgia to the Carolinas. The radio reported incessantly on the efforts to recover bodies in New York and Washington and described the fighter jets streaking over both cities; it rendered the grapplings of a nation in shock. I found it difficult to shake the images of an airplane slamming into the walls of the Pentagon. My father, a career military officer, had been posted there for many years. The walls could not have been ripped open. The building was unassailable. There were so many dead.

In Washington, Secret Service cars tore up and down Connecticut Avenue and, more ominously, patrolled Rock Creek Park and the National Zoo. Antiaircraft batteries were installed near the Washington Monument, and machine guns were everywhere one looked at National Airport. There was the near-constant sound of F-16's flying overhead on their combat patrols. It was an intense time, but a good one as well. Our neighborhood restaurants were packed at night with Washingtonians seeking closer contact with one another. Richard and I went out with friends almost every night. People, even strangers, were gentler for a while. The city was vulnerable. We all were.

In the days and weeks following September 11, Richard became medically practical. He put together a medical kit for the house that contained antibiotics, antivirals, and epinephrine. He divided up reading for the two of us to do: he took anthrax and plague for himself; I was assigned smallpox and botulism. (When I made murmurings that I wanted plague, he laughed and said, "Fair's fair. You got to choose the movie last weekend.") We both read up on the psychiatric complications of antibiotics and antiviral medications, which were not inconsiderable.

The city of government pulled together its people and its agencies. Richard, who had conducted a large study with the Department of Defense to evaluate early treatment intervention in major psychiatric illnesses, was asked by colleagues at the Pentagon to help draw up guidelines for dealing with the psychological and psychiatric consequences of mass violence. At the end of October, on a beautiful fall morning, we drove to Airlie House in Virginia for a meeting put together by the departments of Defense, Health and Human Services, and Justice to frame the response of the federal government to the psychiatric casualties of large-scale terrorist attacks.

We approached the meetings with the same double-channeling that now characterized everything in our lives: one channel of consciousness was on Alert, for the progression of Richard's cancer, and, at a far more distant level of concern, for the threat of another attack on Washington. The other channel was on Normal, for the unthreatened part of our lives. They were separate channels, gliding by each other. On occasion they met, as they did during our days at Airlie House. The countryside was lovely—there were rolled stacks of hay in the fields, and black walnut pods underfoot. We sat on a bench in the gardens, utterly peaceful, as if cancer did not grow in Richard's lungs; as if the meetings we had come to attend were not about the obliteration of minds in the wake of the obliteration of cities.

I listened to Richard's comments during the meetings, struck, as always, by his reasonableness. He argued that we are a resilient species: we made it out of the trees, out of the last Ice Age, through an apocalyptical flood, and out of our mothers' wombs. We would make it now. He made the case, as others did, that the government should not get swept up in programs that sounded good but were not backed by data. The scientific evidence was strong, for example, that interventions such as psychological debriefing did as much harm as good. Yet a cottage industry had evolved to send "debriefers" into areas that had been hit by natural catastrophes such as hurricanes, earthquakes, and floods. Debriefers had gone en masse to New York after the attacks on September 11. Physicians, as Hippocrates had declared, should first do no harm. Richard talked about ways to prevent psychosis and suicide in the psychiatrically vulnerable.

I sat in the back of the room and listened to him. He was dying, but still he was determined to do what he could do to help. I loved listening to him; I loved the way he thought. I loved him. But that night in bed, when I heard him coughing through much of the night, I could not sleep. The world would go on without him, although not as well, but I had no idea what I would do.

Richard's cough came and went, and with it came and

went our anxieties. Shortly after we returned from Airlie House, Richard had his two-month checkup at Hopkins, which was preceded by our usual dread. This time, however, unlike at our earlier visits, there had been no significant tumor growth in his lungs. Ettinger was clearly surprised and delighted by this; we were equally delighted, and stunned. Richard had been following an experimental protocol developed by Judah Folkman at Harvard, taking a combination of medications to starve the blood supply to his tumors and injecting himself twice daily with interferon to strengthen his immune system. He was now well past the survival time predicted for his type of cancer, and we hoped he might be among the newly emerging group of cancer patients whose disease neither worsened nor improved. They lived with their disease. They lived. This possibility, and the possibility of new experimental drugs and vaccine therapy, gave us enough hope to override the intruding presence of his cough, the cold numbers we read in the oncology journals, and the uniformly discouraging second opinions we received from other doctors.

In late autumn, Richard enthusiastically turned his interest and energy to the upcoming Leonid meteor showers. He had been in love with the stars and the skies since he was a young child, when his stepfather had first taken him to Chicago's Adler Planetarium. His stepfather had encouraged him to read about the stars, and this, in turn, had been a powerful motivator for

Richard to overcome his dyslexia. His childhood passion for astronomy was evident still. Astronomers predicted that the meteor storm of November 2001 would be the most spectacular sky event of the twenty-first century. Observers during a typical meteor shower might see ten meteors an hour; this meteor storm promised a thousand an hour, perhaps ten thousand or more. There was no way we were going to miss this night of shooting and falling stars.

We woke up at 4:30 a.m. and drove into Rock Creek Park, which was already thick with cars. Washington may be jaded to human nature, but it keeps itself open to beauty. The meteor showers were magnificent in every way: spectacular bursts of green, white, and blue lights flaming across the sky, mixed with the flashing lights of the AWACS patrolling overhead. Shooting stars exploded in every direction high in the air. How perfect this is, I thought. How perfect it is that we have this, that we are watching this astonishing beauty together. How perfect that Richard is alive to see it. It is a gift for Richard's grace. We caught bits of these falling stars, put them away for the days to come.

Richard talked quietly but passionately about the shooting stars as they rained down over Rock Creek Park. How beautiful they were, he said, how transient. Then he talked about young American soldiers, watching under an Afghan sky. Some would see the Leonids, some would be spotting targets for bombs, and some would be seeing the bombs burst. But, Richard wondered, what would Bin Laden see as he was being hunted down? Did he share the same awe for glowing dust and raining stars?

We sat in the park for a long time, watching the shooting stars and making wishes upon them, kissing with a kind of sweet abandon. Looking at star fields can induce a piercing terror at one's finite place in the universe. This night it did not. It was just Nature at her most ravishingly beautiful, and we saw it together. It was a moment, one bead among many on our wire of time, and I would not exchange it, or our kisses, for anything in the world.

The Christmas season was a whirl of lights and carols and friends. Richard was feeling well, but I think we knew it would be our last Christmas together. Despite or because of this, it was less fraught than the year before. Perhaps we knew to take it as it came; perhaps we had sifted through some of the awful thinking one must do in light of death. But it was a festive time: trimming the tree was a gayer thing, each ornament less weighted with dark sentiment. Most of our evenings were spent by the fire ("Kay," Richard would ask me, "would you like to make one of your special fires?"), and he and I and my mother would talk or listen to carols, have a glass of wine, and stare into the fire, dreamy and happy. The future was not unimportant; it was just put to the side for a while. Richard was dying, my mother was getting older, our dog was white in her muzzle and stiff in her walk, but we took what we had. Our lives were differently precarious, but we knew that this season was one to hold close, and we did.

"Sad?" asked the poet Douglas Dunn about the last days he had with his wife. "Yes. But it was beautiful also. / There was a stillness in the world. Time was out."

As we did every year, we drove through the neighborhood to look at Christmas lights, and on Christmas night we watched, as we always did, *The Bishop's Wife.* Richard nibbled on plum pudding and provided his usual running commentary on why Loretta Young should have run off with Cary Grant instead of staying with David Niven. Each year, I would say, "You're much more like Cary Grant than David Niven." And, because it was true for me, I would say, "Cary Grant wouldn't have had a chance next to you. You're the best-looking man I know."

This Christmas, Richard was frighteningly thin, and he looked his age, which he had never done. His hair was no longer thick or raven black. I leaned over and kissed him and said, "You're still the best-looking man I know."

He smiled at me, but I saw tears in his eyes.

"Really?" he asked.

"By far," I said. "By far."

We settled into our days. The first snow of the season came thick, soft, and gorgeous in mid-January, filling the park and covering our trees and garden. Richard was sleeping more now and eating less, but as long as I was near him when he slept I felt that our small part of the world was good. Richard's two-month evaluation at Hopkins came and went. There was a slight new infiltrate in his left lung, but this did not seem to bother Ettinger. It didn't sound good to me, but I wasn't an oncologist. Ettinger declared Richard's disease "stable" and recommended that his treatment remain the same. Ambinder came into Ettinger's office to visit us, clearly happy to see Richard looking at least reasonably well. Richard said, "You always seem surprised that I'm still alive." Ambinder smiled and didn't deny it.

Richard took me to our neighborhood Italian restaurant for dinner on Valentine's Day. It was a serious and sad evening. It was the only time we discussed what would happen to me after he died, and it was obvious that he had given a great deal of thought to what he would say. He started by telling me how much he loved me and how happy I had made him. He said he wished he could say that he would be keeping an eye out for me once he was gone but, as I knew, he didn't believe in such things. He did believe in the lasting influence of love. You have good friends, family, and colleagues, he said. You have a good doctor and work that is important. You will have to take care of yourself. You will have to take your medication and get your sleep. No one will be around to remind you. It was as though he had rehearsed the speech and did not know what to say next.

"But what will I do without you?" I asked him. "What will I do?"

Richard came over to my side of the table and put his

arms around me. "I don't know," he said. "But you will be all right."

I had not cried in front of Richard since he had been diagnosed with lymphoma nearly three years earlier, but now the tears were streaming down my face. Richard pulled out his Valentine's gifts for me, hoping, I suppose, that what he had gotten for me might help. The first present was an NIH file folder, which had a stylized glass beaker on the front; he had decorated the folder with large red and pink hearts. It looked ridiculous, and I loved it. Inside the folder were two sheets of paper. The first was the dedication page for his manuscript *Cancer Tales.* It was straightforward and very Richard. "To Kay," it read. "Without whom I would not be."

Richard's second gift was a copy of a letter he had written to me more than fifteen years earlier. I was living in London at the time and was in the midst of a deep and unshakable depression. He had called me one night from Washington and been unnerved by the depth of my despair. He wanted to know what he could do to help when I felt so at the end of the world and beyond hope. He said he knew depression clinically but not personally and he was frightened.

I reread his letter, written so long ago now, and thought how far we had come in our understanding of one another, how lucky we had been to have each other, and how his misspellings could still make me smile. "I like your spelling of 'flare' better than the correct one," I told him through my snufflings. He looked at the letter

11/28/85 Thu

Dr. Kay R. Jamison
34 Beaufort Gardens
London S.W.3
England

Dearest K,

I have seen the green ice and the ten minute retreats, but last night I heard total blackness. When I was twelve we visited Mammoth Cave in Kentucky. The guide said that it was twenty degrees darker than total darkness, a statement I have never understood. I still do not understand it scientifically. I have now, however, felt it. It is like a black hole drawing all light into it. On the phone I felt life being sucked out of me threw the wires; gladly given. Unfortunately, there was no conservation of matter and what left me was not to be found in the receptacle on the other end. It was as if there was a total annihilation of substance and energy. It brought back memories of my most primitive childhood nightmare.

Being with you seemed like the only answer. Then I could see it, throw a blanket over it, put a glass of water by the bed, find its lithium, thyroid and if necessary get help. I need some guidelines on the later. I need to know when to worry. Is length of depression or depth the crucial issue or some combination? If I ask you are you taking your medicines, how specific do I need to be? If I ask you are you eating and drinking do I need to ask you calorie by calorie and glass by glass? What will tell me that you are toxic? In Los Angeles I can call Dan Auerbach. Who do I call in London; Anthony Storr, the Darlingtons?

I am not glad the black hole is there but I am glad I have seen it. When you fall in love with a star you accept solar flairs, black holes and all.

Love,

R

and said, "Well, it looks correct to me." A lifetime of dyslexia had not altered his confidence in how certain words should look.

He had always thought of me as an intense star, he said, alluding to the last paragraph. He brought out a small box and gave it to me. "This is for your solar flares and the black holes. And for our shooting stars over Washington." Inside was a gold ring with sixteen small stars on it. He dipped it in my wine and put it on my finger, next to my wedding ring and the gold ring he had given me in Rome.

"To stars," he said.

I reminded him of the quotation from Byron's *Don Juan* that I had used in dedicating one of my books to him: "To those who, by the dint of glass and vapour, / Discover stars, and sail in the wind's eye."

"To you," I said. "To safe sailing."

When I look back on it now, my Valentine's gift to Richard was an absurdly optimistic one. I had made reservations for us to spend a week in Big Sur in early April. We had not been there together and it was something we had always wanted to do. It was improbable, but not impossible, to do it now. The trip would be long but manageable; once in Big Sur, we could read and drive along the coast and mull and enjoy ourselves. We could relax; we could stop time again. Richard expressed concerns about the practicalities but was enthusiastic. When we got home, he sat down with my maps of Big Sur and I watched him with delight. Our trip was something to reach for, a race of hope against death.

Within the month, we knew that we would not go to Big Sur together. Richard was too sick. I told him I planned to cancel my lecture at the University of California at Davis, as well as the trip to Big Sur, but he was vehement that I not do this. "You're exhausted," he said, "and we have a difficult time ahead." I argued that I didn't want to go anywhere without him, but he insisted, and he was right. I *was* exhausted, physically and mentally. For three years I had been taking him to appointments at Hopkins and visiting him when he was in the hospital, sometimes driving from Washington to Baltimore and back twice a day; waiting with him for the results of scans and blood tests, meeting with doctors, requesting consultations, getting prescriptions filled; reading up on his illnesses and treatments; fixing meals and looking after the house. I was hopelessly behind in my work, struggling to maintain my psychological bearings, and trying to keep up his spirits and those of our friends and colleagues. Above all, I was worried sick about him.

We compromised. I would go to Davis for a day to give my talk, and then drive down to Big Sur for two or three days. My mother said she would come to Washington to help look after Richard while I was gone; she also said she strongly agreed with him that I needed a few days off. She told me that I sounded exhausted and that she was worried about me. She felt, like Richard, that Big Sur was exactly what I needed. I felt guilty about leaving and was fearful that Richard would get worse. Terrible things could happen quickly.

Richard and my mother were right. I needed Big Sur. I needed to stand at the edge of the ocean and see the Big Sur coast and the mountains and renew some of what was broken inside of me. Even if that renewal lasted only as long as it would take to get me through Richard's death, it would be an essential thing. Big Sur gave me back some of my spirit, and that, in turn, I gave back to Richard.

I went to Pfeiffer Beach shortly after I got to Big Sur and read the note Richard had given to me before I left Washington. "We wanted to do this for so long and didn't," he had written in his childlike scrawl. "We have done other things. It will not happen in this lifetime and, as you know, I do not believe there is another. But you will know that I am with you in Big Sur. Love, R."

I walked on the beach and read and slept in the sun. And then I slept some more. Only after the first day did I realize how bone-weary I really was. Richard and I spoke every hour or so, and as he said he was feeling better, I felt somewhat less guilty than when I had left Washington. I reread one of my favorite books, *The Once and Future King,* and was struck by King Arthur's resolution and tempered optimism in the face of tragedy. I understood better this time, in the reading and from knowing Richard, the rarity of that kind of strength.

The weather was glorious, which is not usually the case in Big Sur. I ate California artichokes and figs and apricots and walnuts. I filled myself with the sun and the breeze and the ocean and the great tall trees. I looked to the sea and I lifted my eyes to the hills, from which, with the Psalmist, I drew my strength. It passed through my mind that I would not be able to be in Big Sur with anyone other than Richard.

When I returned to Washington, Richard was worse. Within two weeks, he was shorter of breath than he had ever been and he had lost nearly ten pounds. He caught pneumonia. He ate next to nothing and slept more; I watched him lose a bit of his life each day. The intimacy in being together during the approach of death is unimaginable. We knew that what he was going through was final. We lay so close to each other in our bed that we were aware of everything that went on in the other's body. It was a long and private farewell.

In mid-April, Ettinger told us that Richard's disease had "progressed." The way in which he said this gave us no hope. Bob Gallo made arrangements for Richard to enroll in an experimental drug trial at George Washington University Hospital and sent his medical records and scans to a gene therapist at Vanderbilt. Richard was enrolled to participate in the NIH vaccine protocol in the fall, but it seemed unlikely that he would live that long.

He started on Iressa as part of an experimental trial to test the drug's efficacy in patients with lung cancer. It had "shown promise," a phrase we had come to doubt, but there were not many options left. His energy was deteriorating, he spent less time at his computer, and it was only infrequently and with great difficulty that he was able to get up and down the stairs. Friends visited more often now, but their visits were shorter.

We had quiet evenings and somewhat disjointed days from that point on. We waited. We hoped against the reality that we knew. Richard slept more, and I lay next to him and didn't sleep. I read to him for hours a day, although he often fell asleep, and friends and colleagues continued to stream in. At the end of April, Richard and I decided we should have a dinner party for our closest friends to thank them for their friendship and for their extraordinary efforts in trying to save his life. It was our last dinner party, but it was wonderful. I set the table with masses of candles of different heights and azaleas from the garden and made a dinner of papaya with lime and crystallized ginger and figs and salmon and champagne. Everything was alight and beautiful, and the evening was warm with friends who knew exactly what was what.

The next day, I went to Rock Creek Cemetery to pick

out a burial plot for Richard and myself. Richard was too ill to come, but he knew the cemetery because we had been there on several occasions to visit the Saint-Gaudens memorial for Clover Adams. It was the last day of April and there were great blossoming trees everywhere. I called Richard from my cell phone at different sites to describe them to him and to ask which he preferred. We agreed on a place in one of the older parts of the cemetery, near clusters of old trees and within sight of a lily pond. Richard loved the idea of our being near a lily pond in perpetuity and suggested, with a laugh, that I could drop an occasional goldfish into the pond when I came to visit him. It was a sad business.

I did not leave the house unless I absolutely had to. If I was not with Richard, I was distractible and anxious. The only thing that helped was to be with him. In early May, Bob Gallo recommended to Ettinger that Richard try an additional drug, one he had been working on in his laboratory and that had shown antitumor activity. Richard took Gallo's drug along with the Iressa and the Folkman regimen, nibbled at his cottage cheese and canned peaches, and remained in unflappably good spirits. He did not complain. He worked on writing up scientific papers when he had the energy and asked me to read to him when he did not.

There were terrible things to do. Some were small—I bought a black hat with a veil from a saleswoman who was kind enough to match my silence with hers—and others were not. I went to a funeral home to make arrangements and was assisted by a very nice man who asked me if my husband knew I was there. I was surprised by the question, and said, "Yes, of course."

"You would be surprised how many wives don't tell their husbands they are coming here," he said.

Not for the first time or the last, I was grateful to Richard for his directness in dealing with death and his incapacity to deny the inevitable. I picked out a simple birch casket and explained to the funeral director that Richard would just as soon be thrown to the fishes but that I wanted his physical presence for myself, and for how others would remember him. I told him that Richard was a doctor and a scientist who had saved many lives and that I loved him beyond reckoning. I told this man more than I needed to tell him, but then I am sure I was not the first to do this.

In May, Richard and I continued the discussion of funeral plans that we had started in California. Only now we were not on a bench under the sun and we knew that time had run out. Richard was propped up against pillows at the head of our bed and I sat up against the footboard. We discussed friends he wanted to serve as pallbearers and ushers and who should give the eulogies, who should do the readings. A friend of ours, John Harper, who had been the rector of St. John's Church on Lafayette Square, where I had been a parishioner before switching to Christ Church in Georgetown, had been by to visit Richard on several occasions during his illness. He gave Richard tapes of hymns, and indicated to him the ones most often used in funeral services. Richard asked if there was any way he could have all Christmas carols, but the priest suggested this was probably not going to be acceptable. Richard and I just laughed; he was a thorough nonbeliever, but he loved Christmas carols even more than I did.

Richard asked me to read to him the funeral service in *The Book of Common Prayer*, and then asked if there were any biblical passages about medicine or science. I said I did not know, but spoke later with Stuart Kenworthy, the rector of my church, who suggested a reading from the Gospel of Luke. Then we turned to hymns. Richard knew unequivocally that he wanted "Amazing Grace," and had picked out two others he liked from the music John Harper had given him. He asked me what my favorites were so that he would include one that I particularly liked. We lay in bed and listened to the three hymns I suggested and he gave his reactions.

Under the circumstances, he said wryly, he thought he would pass on "How Great Thou Art." He neither liked nor disliked my favorite, "Lead, Kindly Light," so he said he thought he would pass on that one as well. He asked to listen to "Immortal, Invisible, God Only Wise" again and then said, with the honesty of a dyslexic who had engaged in a lifetime war with poetry, "I have no idea what the words mean, but I like the music." So he chose a hymn he knew I loved and one that he did not understand. As he pointed out, he didn't really have to understand it.

We did a run-through of the funeral program. I read from the copy of *The Book of Common Prayer* that we had used in the blessing of our marriage in Los Angeles, and we played the hymns in the order of the program that they would occur. I got out Jessye Norman's recording of "Amazing Grace," which Richard loved, and we listened to it. When it had finished, I looked at Richard, who had a slight smile on his face. "Sounds great!" he said. "Let's do it!" He laughed easily, I less so.

The days and nights did not get any better for Richard. He slept more and, despite oxygen, now and again would gasp for air as a fish will when taken from the sea. He did not respond to either of the experimental drugs and, with that, a cold dread came into the house and stayed. I returned to the funeral home to talk with the man who had assisted me before. He was kind and direct and reassured me, "We will take good care of your husband." They had taken care of Oliver Wendell Holmes and Franklin Delano Roosevelt, he said, and Thurgood Marshall and John F. Kennedy. I told him my husband would be pleased, especially about Thurgood Marshall. I turned to leave.

"We'll see you later," he said.

I tried to respond but my heart had stopped.

It was early June 2002. The foxglove was high in our front garden, and the honeysuckle was climbing every which way over the stone walls. I picked armfuls of pink and white peonies and put them in the bedroom. Never, in seventeen summers with Richard, had I seen so many butterflies as there were now, in this early June. I tried to catch a small white one to keep Richard company, but I couldn't keep up with it. And, as Richard said, I shouldn't have tried. The butterfly ought to be free to fly in the garden.

He said this without envy or regret.

Joy Be the Starlight

We spent most of our last day at home together reading and writing in the room across from our bedroom. Richard worked on a foreword he had agreed to do for a colleague's book and I read. He was very tired, and fell asleep now and again, but it was a good day. A peaceful and private day. I read to him what I had written the day before for my book on exuberance, a habit we had slipped into after he first became ill with lymphoma. I had quoted Robert Louis Stevenson, and he had asked me to read to him from Stevenson's original essay on youth and old age.

I made us a cup of tea and began reading. "We may compare the headlong course of our years to a swift torrent in which a man is carried away," Stevenson had written. "We have no more than glimpses and touches; we are torn away from our theories; we are spun round and round and shown this or the other view of life, until only fools or knaves can hold to their opinions. We take a sight at a condition in life, and say we have studied it; our most elaborate view is no more than an impression."

Richard was intrigued by Stevenson's assertion that no matter how carefully man studied something, his understanding was incomplete, an impression only. He seemed both heartened and disconcerted by the observation, and spoke about partial, shifting knowledge in the context of his own science. The advances in the understanding of schizophrenia and the brain were rapid, but however much was being learned, relatively little was actually known. Much of what was known would not last. He talked at length about how much he regretted dying without being a part of the discoveries to come. He would never know what causes schizophrenia or how to prevent it. He did not know now, he said, most of what would be commonplace science in twenty years.

What he said was true. Discovery is the boon and the chafe of science; much of what is learned will be supplanted by newer findings. There was no good answer to his regrets except to say that the pursuit of new knowledge is reward in its own right and that knowledge begets new knowledge. For those doing medical research, there is the reward that comes from easing pain and saving lives. I reminded him of how deeply he had loved his scientific work and being a doctor, and how much he had improved the lives of those who suffer from schizophrenia and other psychiatric illnesses. He had passed on his enthusiasm, curiosity, and intellectual rigor to the hundreds of young scientists he had trained. For them and for his colleagues, including me, he had been the best possible example of discipline, imagination, and the refusal to give up.

"Perhaps," he said.

Still, he knew that what I said was true. His colleagues and those he had mentored had made clear to him their respect for his science and his character. The impending death of a colleague fosters hyperbole, but the sincerity of the tributes from his peers was obvious.

"Perhaps," he said. "Perhaps."

But he smiled, and his mood was brighter.

Richard did not want to die, but he was not afraid to. He did not want to end his explorations of the brain, but he knew he had had a passionate run. He had used a fine brain to study the brains of those less fortunate, and he had made a difference. He was not lucky to die when he did, but he was lucky to have lived as he lived.

That night, I lay in Richard's arms for a long time, thinking about us, thinking about him. I was peaceful in a way I had not been for months and felt some hope that we might have longer together than we thought. When I woke up in the morning, Richard was gasping for breath.

We drove immediately to George Washington University Hospital, where the doctor who examined him said that both of Richard's lungs had collapsed. In all likelihood, he said, this had happened over a short period of time and, with luck, inserting a chest tube would allow him to breathe more easily. Richard underwent surgery, and I sat with him that night as long as the hospital would permit. He did not look better, however. Indeed, he looked sicker than I had ever seen him look.

When visiting hours were over, the nurse insisted I leave his room. I was deeply unsettled by this; it was, I know now, the primitive distress of an animal being taken from its dying mate. I had worked in hospitals for nearly thirty years, however, and saw the need for rules. Rules matter, except when they should matter least.

As I got up to leave, Richard said, "I love you, sweetheart."

"I love you, too," I said. I reached over to kiss him good-night. "See you in the morning." It was the same exchange we had had every night for nearly twenty years, but this time it was our last.

At four o'clock the next morning, a doctor in the hospital's intensive care unit called to tell me that Richard's health had deteriorated and he was in grave condition.

"I think it is important that you come to the hospital as quickly as possible, Mrs. Wyatt," the doctor continued. "His chances are not good."

My drive to the hospital was a nightmare, my half-sprint to the ICU worse. When I finally found Richard's room and saw him, I knew he was going to die. He was unconscious and connected to a tangle of tubes, monitors, and a ventilator. Although unconscious, he was struggling with the ventilator because of earlier damage caused by radiation to his esophagus.

Richard never regained consciousness. His face

swelled from the fluids he was given to fight infection and to keep his blood pressure elevated. By the second day in the ICU, he was unrecognizable. The doctors extended next to no hope for his survival. Even if he survived the wildfire sepsis, they said, it was hard to imagine, with his diseased lungs, how he could ever get off the ventilator. I watched the numbers on his monitors lurch about, and with them lurched my moods.

Stuart Kenworthy, the rector of my church, came by the hospital to visit, and I was surprised by how much better I felt after talking with him. It was consoling in an ancient, essential way. Perhaps because priests see human life from baptism to death, they have both a more profound and a more pragmatic perspective on death than others do. He was certainly more comfortable in an ICU than I was. I found it hard to deal with the physical changes in Richard and told Stuart that I doubted I would ever be able to get rid of the images of Richard's bloated face. It was the least of matters, but it was one that haunted me. He said that I would, in time. He suggested I put my favorite photographs of Richard around the house and that eventually I would remember him as he had been. It was good advice, practical, and it worked.

After Stuart left, I picked up my copy of *The Book of Common Prayer,* looked up the Order for the Burial of the Dead, and started to read. "I am the resurrection and the life, saith the Lord," it began, and I thought: Not yet; I will hear this soon enough. I closed the book. But then, as minds will do during such times, I suppose, I sought out the past to prepare for and provide solace for what was to come.

Standing by Richard's bedside, I thumbed through the prayer book and read aloud to him one last time. It was a prayer the priest had read to us in Los Angeles. "Let their love for each other be a seal upon their hearts. Let it be a mantle about their shoulders, and a crown upon their foreheads. Bless them in their work and in their companionship; in their sleeping and in their waking; in their joys and in their sorrows; in their life and in their death."

The words had meant a very different thing to me when life was what we had and death was unimaginable. I had heard then *love* and *companionship* and *joys*. Now I heard the force of different words, *sorrows* and *death*. But I heard *love* as well.

The attending physician came to me not long after and said, "Mrs. Wyatt, we need to talk about what your husband would have wanted done." He was direct and kind; he was very professional. We went through the details of Richard's advance directives, which were unambiguous, and decided upon the medical conditions for removing life support. I went to a hotel nearby to get a few hours of sleep, afraid to risk getting manic, desperately hoping he would live through the night so that I would be with him when he died.

He lived through the night. The next morning, the

ICU doctors asked me if I wanted to stand in with them on their rounds as they discussed Richard's medical situation. I listened to what they said, appreciative that the clinical discussion made it clear that his death was inevitable. He had organ failure in his heart, lungs, kidneys, liver, and whatever else there was that could fail. His pupils were fixed and dilated. There was no hope for survival. We went through his advance directives again and I made the decision to have his blood pressure medications and ventilator withdrawn. The decision, which was a straightforward one, seemed anticlimactic to the preceding days of unsustainable, chaotic monitor numbers. He was, in reality, already dead. It remained for me to give sanction to it. I did this with cold fear.

An ICU, of necessity, is a well-lit and exposed place, but the nurses did the best they could to lend privacy to Richard's death. What they did and their way of doing it was thoughtful and habitual. They removed the trails of plastic tubing and the bleating machines, drew the curtains around his bed, and dimmed the lights. He was alive, but scarcely and not for long. I had no idea what to say to him other than to repeat, again and again, "Thank you for such happiness."

To myself I said, *I want my husband back.* It became a mantra over the weeks to come. *I want my husband back.*

I looked at Richard's body, which had been through so much for so long, and I was, by the grace of books, given the gentlest of images. I remembered Hazel, the great-hearted and open-minded leader of the band of rabbits in *Watership Down,* a book both Richard and I loved. When Hazel died, he simply left his body on the edge of a ditch and then ran off free of his tiredness, through the woods and into a field of primrose. Hazel's fairness and self-assurance had always reminded me of Richard—both in how he lived and how he died—and the image of Hazel's light taking-leave-of-life was genuinely comforting.

It was the beginning of my true knowing of the consolation of language. I would soon learn that the images that drift in and out of one's mind during grief are not always kind. The mind can cut both ways; it can throw up memories that disturb or delight, relieve or agitate. The mind is unpredictable. I should have known this, of course. But, whatever was to come, the image of Hazel's release was a gift when I most needed it.

I put my head on Richard's shoulder and broke down completely. Then I kissed him good-bye and went into another room to complete the paperwork that goes with death.

The rest of the day filled with the practicalities of autopsy permissions, funeral arrangements, whom to call, and what to do. Why to do it was not an option of thought. That night, the night that Richard died, my mother, my brother, and Richard's and my close friends sat outside, on long grassy grounds in Maryland, and drank mint juleps before dinner. It was a beautiful, early June evening, and given the circumstances, we had a strangely lovely time. Despite the awfulness of it all, everyone drew together and reminisced and laughed. We were so different, Richard and I, and that made for much of the laughter. As it always had. My friend Jeremy ordered a bottle of champagne and offered a toast to Richard, and we raised our glasses: first to him, and then to Richard and me, and then to the band of friends that we were. Our friends and family had made Richard's and my last years not just bearable but exceptional. They would continue to do so in the months to come; they would make his death endurable.

A colleague of mine from Hopkins and his wife, good friends to both Richard and me, came down from Baltimore to have dinner the next night. They brought not only kindness and shared memories, but also sleeping medication. The latter was to avert my becoming manic during a time when I was likely to lose sleep. My colleague made it easy for me. Instead of my having to call one of my doctors and wait at a pharmacy, which I was unlikely to do, he took it into his hands to get a prescription filled. It was a small act of kindness but enormously important. I benefited from the fact that many of my friends and colleagues were not only practicing psychiatrists, but specialists in mood disorders as well. Most particularly, I benefited from their compassion. Over the coming months, they called me often to make sure I was getting enough sleep, that I was not manic, not depressed.

There were so many things to do. Someone from the

funeral home called to ask me to bring over clothes for Richard, a task I found abhorrent. I picked out a shirt I had gotten for him in London, the silk tie he had worn the day we married, and gray slacks. I could not imagine why I was picking out such uncomfortable, formal clothes for him to wear, but that seemed to be what one did. It was dreadful and pointless and I cried the entire time. Days later, when Richard's body finally was delivered to the funeral home, I had to formally identify his body. He was scarcely recognizable to me. I signed yet another paper of death and asked them to close the casket and not allow anyone else to view his body.

The funeral was held in St. John's Church in Georgetown, a few blocks from my own church, which was being restored. The church was packed and the service beautiful. The soloist sang "Amazing Grace" magnificently, and I wondered how closely Richard had attended to the words. I thought I knew the hymn well, but it was only in hearing it sung on that afternoon, in that way, and for Richard, that I heard the words *dangers* and *grace* as they were meant, and that grace would lead him home. I don't think he ever thought of himself in terms of grace, but I did. Or at least a particular kind of grace. Certainly, Richard would not have thought of "going home" in any hymnal sense, but it was a lovely rendition all the same. And it was for him.

Bob Gallo and Jim Watson gave eulogies bearing witness to Richard as a scientist, a doctor, and a man of kindness. To my delight, Bob also recounted an evening not long before when several of us had gone out to dinner together and Richard had said to me in front of everyone and from out of nowhere, "I love you. You're so beautiful." Bob said then and at the funeral that Richard had a way of raising the bar for romantic behavior.

My brother approached the pulpit slowly. I saw his eyes glance down at Richard's coffin and then, after fingering his tie, something he often does when putting his thoughts together, he straightened his back, placed his notes on the lectern, and began his eulogy. He conveyed our family's condolences to Richard's children and his former wife. He thanked Richard's doctors and colleagues. Then he talked about the photograph in the funeral program. It had been taken the day that Richard and I got married in the Shenandoah Valley, he said. He and my mother had watched Richard, who, unlike me "generally moved in a quiet and deliberate way," literally run up the stairs of the Winchester County Court House, where he had waited, at the top of the landing, with a look of "pure delight" and impatience. It had been, my brother said, "a marvelous moment and a magical day."

It *had* been a magical day. The Shenandoah Valley town where we got married had changed sides seventy times during the Civil War, which, Richard noted, was enough to give one pause. He and I had spent several weekends together in the Shenandoah Valley and were drawn to marry there by romantic memories and the beauty of the great oaks and birches, apple trees and hickories. When I was young, I had raced horses flat out on summer hunts in the Shenandoah Valley and taken horses swimming in the river. It was not far from Washington and, as Richard insisted, we could play Paul Robeson's "Shenandoah" on our way there and back. Which we did, repeatedly. It was a wonderful place to marry; it was a perfect day. The four of us—my mother, my brother, Richard, and I—drove back to Washington after the ceremony was over and had champagne and a quiet dinner in Georgetown. We were impossibly happy.

Later that night, Richard and I made love for the first time as husband and wife. Afterward, he turned to me and said gently, "Good night, Mrs. Wyatt."

I, lulled by sex and happiness, on the cusp of sleep, thought: How beautiful, how strange, how marvelous.

"Good night, Dr. Wyatt," I murmured back.

There was a pause. Then I felt his body next to mine, shaking with laughter.

"You can call me Richard," he said.

And so I had gone to sleep on my wedding night, laughing out loud and hopelessly in love. We understood that life had its bounds, but on that night we believed that time would be generous to us, as love had been.

How odd to smile during Richard's funeral. He was dead and I was smiling to myself. Grief does that. Laughter lies close in with despair, numbness near by acuity, and memory with forgetfulness. I would have to get used to it, but I didn't know this at the time. All I knew, as I sat in Thomas Jefferson's church next to Richard's coffin, was that memory had given pleasure first, and then cracking pain.

I turned to the back of the funeral program and read the words I had chosen for Richard. They were from "Love Song," by the Scottish poet Joseph Macleod:

Your touch will plot us wise,
your quiet keep it true;
and joy be the starlight
to what we have to do.

I wanted stars for him, and quiet. I wanted joy for us.

I rode with Richard's body to Rock Creek Cemetery, a lonely and strange ride in the pelting rain. The grave attendants had left, the weather being so foul, and the committal service was held in the small parish church. The ancient words gave comfort: "Earth to earth, ashes to ashes, dust to dust," and when they were done, I put yellow tulips on his casket and kissed him through the birch wood. Richard was not near, but he was not yet gone. Then I walked out into the downpour.

The next morning was as fair as the day before had been foul. It was a morning filled with sun, a good day, if the day we committed Richard's body to the earth could be such a thing. The grave was very deep, a sharp reminder that space was being kept for my own coffin. I looked down at Richard's coffin and tried to think of a way to say good-bye to him, but my mind would not let me do this in peace. It would not give me the words to say good-bye, the clarity to say "I love you." It threw up terrible questions and images instead.

What was the last thing Richard had thought before losing consciousness? I tormented myself. What had he felt as they hooked him up to the IVs and monitors, as they injected him, prodded him, forced a tube down his throat? Was it fear? Was it pain? Did he have any chance to use his mind to think of other things? To hope? Why had I not stayed with him in his room, when I knew he was so ill? Why did I choose then to conform to mindless rules, to do what a nurse insisted?

I did not know how to stop my mind, except to reach for thoughts and images that might compete. I thumbed through *The Book of Common Prayer* again, and found the second of the wedding prayers we had used to celebrate our marriage. It had been such a good day, such a day of happiness.

"Give them wisdom and devotion in the ordering of their common life," the priest had said to us. "That each may be to the other a strength in need, a counselor in perplexity, a comfort in sorrow, and a companion in joy."

I would miss my counselor in perplexity, my companion in joy. I would miss his ordering of our common life.

PART THREE

OF SOMETHING LOST

The yule-log sparkled keen with frost,
No wing of wind the region swept,
But over all things brooding slept
The quiet sense of something lost.

—ALFRED, LORD TENNYSON

Wildflowers and Granite

In the weeks after Richard died, time moved erratically; memory was capricious. I could make no sense of how my mind worked and soon stopped trying. Shock protected my heart, but porously. I knew it must be shock because I got done what I needed to do. I knew the protection was porous because, when I was least expecting it, a memory would bring me to my knees. I had then the cold horror: Richard is dead. I will not see him again. There may have been rules that determined which memories came unawares, or when they would choose to strike, but I never discerned them. Logic came from the world without, not the one within.

Practical matters and tradition dictated the things that needed to be done after his death. I had only to find a place to start and an inevitable progression would emerge. I started by sorting through Richard's things. I knew this would be a minefield to negotiate, but it was what made sense to me at the time: I would go through his desk, his books and clothes, his papers and financial files, and the medications that hadn't worked well enough.

Richard's desk seemed the obvious place to start, although I soon found it to be too much him to continue and stopped not long after I had started. There was a glass bowl containing a tangle of keys to our house, his offices and the wards at St. Elizabeths and NIH, to his labs, his car. Most of the keys were labeled, but who would find that helpful now? His wallet lay on his desk; I found it impossible to pick it up, impossible not to. In it was a photograph of me with long hair and a laugh I would never have again. There were credit cards, a driver's license, and—in an unusual exercise in the poetry of everyday life—a medical license stating that Richard was "duly registered to practice the healing art in the District of Columbia." Had that phrase, "the healing art," caught Richard's attention? I would not know. I could not ask him.

I went restlessly from room to room in the house, finally settling again in his study. I stared at his books for a long while and pulled down a few, incapable of facing them in any systematic way. Anna Freud's *The Ego and the Mechanisms of Defense* loomed out at me: Had it always been there? What was it doing on Richard's bookshelf? He was a die-hard psychopharmacologist and biological psychiatrist. I opened the cover and there it was, a bookplate marked "Ex Libris Richard J. Wyatt, M.D." It was true, then; Richard had had a copy of Anna Freud's book in his possession. Strange. I was oddly reassured to see that there was not a single margin note or underlined phrase. *Basic Methods in Molecular Biology* and *The Mesocorticolimbic Dopamine System,* on the other hand, were copiously notated and their margins filled with his scrawl. I felt better; the Richard I had known reemerged a bit. I quit his bookshelves when I came across the section of books he had written or coauthored; I wasn't up for too much Richard too soon. It was beginning to be clear that with Richard dead, work and books and ideas were not going to be such fun again; I was not going to be able to walk across the hallway and ask him a question about science or medicine. Or lure him into bed. He was dead.

There was no avoiding Richard in our own house, of course. His file cabinets were everywhere and their contents gave me some pleasure; they also ripped my heart apart. Five entire file drawers were filled to brimming with letters and cards and other bits and pieces I had sent or given to him over the years. I was touched by the fact that he had kept these things and somehow relieved that he had had concrete evidence of how much I loved him. I had never questioned that he knew how much I loved him, but he was not there to allay my sudden insecurity. Had I shown him often enough, and well enough, how much he meant to me? It was too late now.

I found the notes he had kept about my illness in another file drawer: chartings of my moods and medications, lithium research papers with margin notes and queries, pages photocopied from books about mania.

Detailed, reassuring. Who will do it now? Who will ever care enough, or be knowledgeable enough, to do it again? Into one folder, labeled "Suicide/MDI," Richard had slipped a letter I had written him, with one paragraph bracketed in red ink: "Thursday is the anniversary of my almost having killed myself," I had written. "For the life of me, I cannot understand why this day is so important to me but—always—it is tied up with my prayers, failures, survivals and—always—I have a glass of wine and a moment to myself and a toast 'To Life.' All this by way of saying it is a season of grim memories and I wish I could be held very tight. But knowing you makes it so much less bad, so much less lonely."

I sat down and reread the letter.

In all our years together, Richard never failed to remember this dark anniversary. It was a day we marked each year with a glass of wine and a toast to life. Later, I would find this date marked in his appointment book with "Kay." So many things were going to end.

In a different file drawer, I found photocopies of letters Richard had sent to me over the years. It was too painful to read beyond the first two or three, so I stopped and put them into a box that I thought I would open in a few months' time, after my emotions had settled. I did not open the box for five years. The first letter, which I did read, was one Richard had written to me about why he loved me. "The smile and laugh light up the room," he had written. "But the reflectiveness holds my attention. There is self-confidence without arrogance, vulnerability without weakness. There is self-preservation, but kindness. Insight is with humor, perception with appreciation, and intellect with judgment. The judgment rules but intuition is the guide." Was this how he had seen me? It must have been; it was addressed to me and signed by him. I had forgotten this letter and I loved having it now. Will any man love me this way again? What will I do without him? *I want my husband back.*

I dreamed that night that I was meeting Richard for dinner and I saw him across the room. I got up from the table and went to him, relieved and filled with joy. Something made me hesitate, though, and made me ask: "Are you dead?"

He said, very gently, "Yes," and I woke up sobbing, bereft, alone.

I should have known that Richard, creator of under-the-bedcovers Easter egg hunts, and author of countless original acts of love, would have left me help to wend my way through grief. He did. On the second day of going through his things, I found a letter under his computer, handwritten, on the precarious downward slant his handwritten letters seemed always to take. He said in it how lucky we had been to find each other and that he had learned from me how to love. And, he wrote, perhaps I had found some relief from my restlessness and passing despairs. He said that he was grateful for the extra time we had had together and that, until the past few years, he had always assumed he loved me more than I loved him. Not because I didn't love him, he said, but because love was new to him and not to me. "In the past years, however," he ended his letter, "I have seen your love in everything you have done for me. I love you more than you can know."

I sat in his study, with his note in my hands, trying to think what I had done for him that anyone else would not have done. I couldn't think of anything, except perhaps to make transparent my utter delight in his company, and to provide an ampleness of passion and laughter. The love had always been there. It had come and remained without effort, as a star moves in the course that has been set for it.

Two additional envelopes, which I came across under the large box that held his medications, contained cash and explanatory notes. The first was to pay for a birthday present he had charged to a credit card. The gift he had ordered, a pair of aquamarine earrings to match the bracelet he had designed for me in California the year before, arrived at our house a few days after his death, days shy of my birthday.

In the other envelope, Richard had put enough cash for me to buy a basset puppy once Pumpkin, our fourteen-year-old basset hound, died. He had felt for some time that we should get another dog because Pumpkin was old, and he worried that I would be devastated by her death. I had resisted, thinking Pumpkin was used to being the only dog and would find it hard to adapt to another animal in the house.

Certainly, Pumpkin needed consoling during the weeks after Richard died. For days she moped around the house and slept next to Richard's empty reading chair. I could scarcely look at his chair, remembering him reading or tapping away on his laptop, or thinking about our afternoons when I read to him as the sun filled the room. Finally, after several days, I thought to sit in his chair myself, which helped Pumpkin adjust to his absence. I realized that Richard would have figured out what to do in a few minutes' time. It would not have taken him days, as it did me.

Pumpkin had been hopelessly smitten with him. After all, as Richard had often said to our friends, she was a female. And females were drawn to him. He liked to recount our naming of her as an example of this. Pumpkin had come into our life as a ten-week-old puppy and, at the beginning, had a somewhat conflicted relationship with Richard. He had not wanted a dog to begin with and was initially adamant that she not sleep in our bedroom with us. It was bad enough that she jumped up on the couch in his study, he said, but he'd be damned if he was going to pay for her to get up on another psychiatrist's couch because she had been traumatized by some primal scene she had witnessed in our bedroom. It was always disconcerting to hear Richard express a psychoanalytic thought, usually a lingering remnant of his Harvard residency; it meant, among other things, that he was unlikely to change his mind.

In fact, he warmed to her over time. When she was a puppy, still with pink pads on her paws and ears so long that she tripped over them, he nicknamed her "Vicious," a name he continued to use until he died. Pumpkin, who was morbidly shy and the gentlest of bassets, was incapable of anything resembling aggression. Richard persisted in calling her Vicious, and one day suggested putting our competing names for her to the test. We should be objective, he said. Scientific. He sat at one end of the living room and I sat at the other. Then he dropped Pumpkin down midway between us.

"You call her," he said.

"Come here, Pumpkin," I called out to her. She sat, head cocked, listening to my voice. With basset hounds, there is a random correlation between what is asked of them and what is done. She sat expectantly; only her tail moved.

Richard smiled.

"Here, Vicious," he cajoled her. "Come to Richard."

She padded over to him straightaway.

"Science has spoken," he said. "I rest my case."

On our wedding night, I had asked Richard to sit in the living room while I gathered up the first part of my wedding present for him. This came in the form of Pumpkin, and it had been designed to counter his complaint that, unlike the other dogs we came across in the park, she did not know how to do any tricks. This was true, largely because I had never seen the point in teaching her any.

I thought that teaching Pumpkin to do a trick for Richard might cut down on his comments about her inability to learn and my inability to teach. She and I practiced fastidiously in the days leading up to the wedding, and after Richard and I returned from the Shenandoah Valley, I brought her into the living room, white satin bow around her neck, and waved a dog biscuit in front of her nose.

"Speak," I said. She barked immediately. We both looked over to Richard for his approval. There was silence instead, then a smile appeared on his face.

"Great," he said. "The best thing about the dog was that she never barked, and now you've taught her how."

To underscore his point—I had forgotten to give her the dog biscuit she had earned—she started barking frenetically and unceasingly. And then, relentlessly, she bayed.

"Brilliant job, Vicious," said Richard, laughing. "Now leave." She went to her bed and we to ours.

Now, sitting in my reading chair, facing Pumpkin, who was sleeping in Richard's, I realized that it was not that I didn't want to go on without him. I did. It was just that I didn't know *why* I wanted to go on. It would have to be an act of faith.

In the weeks after Richard's funeral, I tried to read the hundreds of condolence letters I had received, but I found it hard to read more than one or two at a time. His friends and colleagues wrote wonderfully about him; their observations were perceptive and generous and brought him, for a moment or two, back to life. But this hurt as often as it helped. The characteristics that others most often ascribed to him—"private," "unassuming," "gentle," "charming"—were ones that I most associated with him as well. And most missed. Many commented on his wit and his generosity to junior colleagues. Several European scientists invoked the word *civilized,* which he would have liked enormously. When the solution to schizophrenia was found, wrote one colleague, Richard's legacy would be complete. I wish he could have read these letters; I wish he could have known how strong and consistent the thread of qualities was, how much respect he had commanded for his mind and for his ways, for how he had dealt with death. "At a time when so many people would justifiably have limited their scope to their own affliction," wrote a friend and colleague, "his mind was still ranging across the universe, searching for curiosities and making observations."

Many were kind enough to express their belief that I had brought Richard great happiness, and I found this genuinely consoling. Jonathan Glover, the British philosopher, wrote, "If I knew enough chemistry, I would know the name for a compound made from two very different chemicals—you and he were that sort of unit." I loved the image, and thought about chemicals that might fit his notion. My mind was slow and muddled, however, and I could not think past lithium and rubidium, elements I had written about and that were opposite in many of their properties. But they would not unite in the way I wanted them to, better together than apart. Richard, I realized, would have come up with something quickly; it would have been clever. Richard is dead.

Richard is dead. Richard, lover of chemicals, lover of stars, would have delighted in the lines of poet Robert Crawford: "All the chemicals that make up our bodies," he wrote, "first emigrated here from far, raw stars." I have Richard now, in far emigrant bits. It is a raw consolation, but a consolation nonetheless.

Most of the condolence letters described Richard, rather than offering advice about how to deal with his being dead. This was just as well. Short of the banal, there was little anyone could meaningfully suggest. Death trumps everything. Two of Richard's former professors from Hopkins, themselves married, wrote words that were true, and their truth became more apparent over time: "We know love makes a difference," they said, "and we send love."

The advice I took most to heart, however, was from a friend of mine, a poet, who spoke of the futility of advice. "I've always handled similar emergencies very badly by working and drinking myself into states of stupor and desolation," he wrote. "If I say that I think it's probably best to get out and about then I know I haven't a leg to stand on. I'll excuse myself from my own worthless advice by saying Everyone's Different. I'm thinking of you, and hoping you're all right." I wasn't all right, but it helped to know that he was thinking of me and that he understood the limitations of words and advice.

I went often to Richard's grave. The day after he was buried, I took tiger lilies from the garden and put them on the red clay earth that topped his grave. I brought him white and apricot-colored honeysuckle, and hydrangeas and petunias as well, which gave beauty and a bit of home to the stark mound of dirt. The water lilies in the pond nearby were high-stalked and yellow. I looked carefully, but there were no goldfish. Richard would smile at the possibilities, I thought. In the weeks to come, the top earth settled on his grave, and I settled into a way of being there. Each armful of flowers that I brought—the last sprigs of honeysuckle, black-eyed Susans, rose of Sharon—left a mark of life, a trace of loveliness. They died, but he is dead. We all die. There is a naturalness to this.

One morning—during the early weeks, when I still spoke aloud to him—I said, "I missed you, sweetheart, when it rained so hard last night. I missed you this morning, when it was no longer raining. I missed you, wondering if the rain would begin again." And then I stopped. I could not bear to think of him alone, so deep in the ground. So unaware of the rain and how much I missed him.

It was peaceful, all the same, and I imagined that soon the grave-tenders would put sod on top of his grave and perhaps I could plant a tree or flowers. I like being here, I thought. I like his company. There was something good and deep that compelled me to his grave, to keep company with him, to comprehend who we had been and what we would become. We had been together in one way, alive and sensate; this had changed. I would have to imagine and invent, as he did, in order for us to have a different way of being together. I would have to know him differently. We would not grow old together—this was implicit in everything I knew and felt; it was among the more terrible realities of his death—but something would survive. I would make it so.

One afternoon, when I got to Richard's grave, I saw that it had been covered with fresh earth, used to fill in the area that had settled. This had raised his grave to the level of the surrounding ground. Everything now seemed final. Richard was no longer among the newly dead; his grave had lost its recent look. Now he was only one of the cemetery's many dead: less new, more permanent. He was freshly dead to me, but not to nature and the parish grounds.

Soon his gravestone was in place and it felt good to lean against it, to trace his name in the granite. It was late summer and the leaves were beginning to come down. In no time at all, they would be heavy on his grave. I faced toward his headstone. I had assumed his head was in that direction, but I dropped a breath when I realized I did not know if this was actually true. I didn't know where on Richard I was standing and it unmoored me. Why did it matter? It just did. It mattered a great deal. I had to distract myself from my morbid thoughts. I went to my car and retrieved my *Field Guide to Eastern Trees* and took it back to Richard's grave. He would like my being a bit more systematic about Nature than I ordinarily am. I could put aside my gruesome thoughts and think of oaks and sycamores.

On my birthday, a week after Richard's funeral, my mother and I drove to the cemetery. She took a lily and a white rose to put on his grave, and I took pink zinnias, honeysuckle, and purple petunias. We both stood there, quiet and hurting. Mother looked unbearably sad—she and Richard had been very close—and I wanted to comfort her; she had done this so often for me. I could not think of anything to say, however; at least nothing that was true. We stood in silence.

"He took such good care of you," she said finally.

Of course, I thought. She must wonder how I will go on without him, *if* I can go on without him. They had shared their worries about me and, similar to each other in habits of restraint, had laughed about my expansive notions of life. Now, everything had changed. She felt anew her old responsibilities. I put my arm around her and told her that I would be fine. I believed this, and I believed it enough for her to believe it.

"I'll miss him," she said softly.

That evening, I put on my new aquamarine earrings from Richard and joined my friends and family in a birthday celebration for which I had no heart. Afterward, my mother suggested we watch a videotape of a talk that Richard had given several years earlier. He had been asked to speak about what it was like to be married to someone with manic-depressive illness. The three of us had watched the tape shortly after he had given the talk and then it had been put aside. I didn't know if it was a good idea or not, but Mother seemed eager to watch it, and, as I remembered, in the talk he had said repeatedly how wonderful she was. My mother, the least vain person I have ever known, wanted to hear this directly from Richard. For my part, I wanted to see Richard as he had been when well, but I was wary. Still, I had to do it sometime.

It was an unsettling, good thing to have done. It was disturbing to see what I no longer had, but reassuring to know that I had had it for as long as I did. In the videotape, Richard talked about me with love and bemusement. He described my awful moods with tolerance, my euphorias and absurd enthusiasms with warmth and affection. He recounted our first Christmas together, when we argued over whether our tiny tree really needed a dozen strands of lights. He had thought me extravagant; I had thought him incapable of grasping the idea that there was no such thing as too many Christmas lights or too much joy.

He made it clear that it was hard on our relationship when I was agitated or irritable, but he made it as clear that he felt our relationship was well worth it. He spoke in a collective sense of how *we* dealt with my illness, how *we* managed it. He said that it was important to be supportive of my strengths and not too hard on my weaknesses. He talked about how much he loved the passions of my mind, and related in detail how, the evening before, I had read to him about elephants and their amazing ways. He didn't back away from how difficult it was to live with a sometimes tumultuous illness, but he gave more weight to love than to disease. As he always had. I watched Richard, handsome and smart and alive, and it broke my heart for missing him. It broke my heart, but it gave me courage as well. I had that man's love, I thought to myself. I had his respect; he desired me. I was lucky. But now what? I didn't know I could hurt so much.

Richard's presence in the weeks and months to come was in shards of memory that came from nowhere and found their mark. His presence was in his absence. It was in my restless turning to him at night, in my seeking places out, not thinking, that prompted memories of shared times, or conjured his ways. I walked to the National Zoo one morning, thinking to distract myself from my life, and ended up at the zebra yard. What was it that made me think of Richard when I was looking at the zebra looking at me? It had slipped my mind. Of course: our first date had been at the zoo, and we had studied the zebras. Did I know that zebras' stripes were different, not only zebra to zebra, but from left to right on the same zebra? Richard had asked me. I did not. I did not know about the left-to-right asymmetry.

"Well, let's see if it's true," he had said.

I was about to learn a great deal more about zebras than I would have chosen to learn. They bark and they whinny, Richard told me with delight. They like tall grasses; they run like the wind. They have amazing, *really* amazing, stripes. We turned to the issue of stripes and, for half an hour or so, in the pages of the notebook Richard carried in his pocket, we mapped out the taperings, widths, and curvings of the stripes in front of us. I began to fall in love with Richard over that zebra.

So there I stood, two decades later, laughing and crying in front of a zebra, trying to recapture the alchemy of Richard's mind and sense of wonder. I couldn't, not as fully as I would have liked, but it was no accident that I had ended up at the zebra yard. My mind sought out its own saving salt, as an animal will seek it in a field. My mind knew what it needed to keep well, to stay alive. The quirks and curiosities that inhabited Richard's mind came unbidden into mine, and with them came life.

When Richard was in the hospital for his bone marrow transplant, I had read to him, from *Wind, Sand and Stars,* Saint-Exupéry's account of his forced landing onto the Sahara. "Our home is yet in truth a wandering star," he had written. "I had kicked against a hard, black stone, the size of a man's fist, a sort of molded rock of lava incredibly present on a bed of shells a thousand feet deep. A sheet spread beneath an apple-tree can receive only apples; a sheet spread beneath the stars can receive only star-dust. Never had a stone fallen from the skies made known its origins so unmistakably."

The traces of Richard's mind that drifted into my own were likewise unmistakable. They could only be from Richard. I came to welcome these times when his imagination wandered into mine. They kept him alive to me and necessary. They kept me tethered to him, as I had been for so long. I did not want to be free of him yet. Why would I?

I returned to Hopkins a month after Richard died and found that it had lost some of its magic for me. The competence and quickness of mind I so loved in my colleagues, and the Oslerian tradition of medicine that defined the character of the hospital, had been eclipsed by Richard's illness and the dread that had been yoked to our every visit to his Hopkins doctors. Richard and I had had such an uncomplicated love for Hopkins; it was muddied now by the failure of his treatment. The love would come back in time, I knew, but it would be more complex. The excellence of his medical care had stood against a disease that was going to win. This juxtaposition was one I would come to see more in my own field, and it had the effect of making me understand Hopkins better and appreciate it more.

My first day back at the hospital was difficult. It was reassuring to return to a world I knew and where people made their caring clear. But after giving a talk to the residents, I had to leave. Life went on, teaching went on, science and good doctors went on. I couldn't. Not this first day. I was at sixes and sevens. I couldn't go back in time, but neither could I move forward. I hadn't then what I needed to be a part of a high-energy endeavor. As I passed by the cancer center, I felt a wave of revulsion. I wanted to run past the graveyard and to forget all that had happened there.

I was restless in everything that I did. It was not the unbearable agitation of mania but, instead, an anxious fluttering that had attached itself to my grief. I walked and walked and then walked some more in an attempt to allay the disquiet. It worked, but not well. I left dinner parties midway through and seldom made it to the end of a film or a concert. My reading was fitful. I started, put aside, and picked up again a wide assortment of books. Each time it was the same. I read a chapter or two and then put the book aside. I started to reread *Watership Down,* thinking to reenter the book Richard and I had read aloud together, but I became anxious, knowing what lay in store for the rabbits. Neither fiction nor nonfiction brought me the escape I hoped for.

My years of dissembling when depressed, of persuading others that I was fine when I was not, turned out to be useful in navigating the no-man's-land between my grief and others' queries and concerns. It took far longer to reconfigure myself after Richard's death than I thought it would, and certainly longer than most people allow. A colleague, not someone distinguished for his sensitivity, asked me, after Richard died, to review a paper for a psychiatric journal. "My husband just died," I found myself snapping.

"It's been three months," he said.

And so it had.

Time means different things to different people. To some in the BlackBerry scramble, three months is long enough. I was inhabiting a slower and more confused world, with a different experience of time altogether. I could not imagine turning from my inward life and sadness to the cold-blooded thinking necessary to do a scientific review. I wanted time to myself with Richard. Soon enough, I would have to enter into the rest of my life without him. This was a time between times, and I did not want to leave it before I had to.

I seemed well enough to my colleagues and friends, and I wasn't depressed. This, together with the fact that I had a horror of weighing heavy on those I knew, made it hard for them to know how distressed I really was. I don't know why I kept such hurt to myself—I wish I had not—but I did not want others to see how much I missed Richard. There was a pressure, as well, or I felt there to be a pressure, to assuage the anxiety of others. A slight measure of sadness was fine, but it was better to leaven it a bit with laughter or reassurance, or by changing the subject. I did admit to a few friends that it was hard, and that, for me, was a major admission. I have always found it difficult to ask others for help, and this was the first time in my life that I was aware of reaching out with my heart so obviously upon my sleeve. So I reached out, but I didn't.

Thankfully, and understandably, people moved on with their lives, and I think I made it easier for them to do so. I am glad I did this; I regret that I did this. I wanted to say, I am hurting more than you can know. But I didn't. I laughed, I colluded, but some of me moved forward with them.

One day, two boxes of Richard's personal effects from NIH arrived at the house. I sat on the floor, sifting through the contents, aching. I didn't know what I would find; it was a bit like Christmas, but not really. In the first box, there were two photographs Richard had kept on his desk: one was a picture that my brother had taken of the two of us on the day we married; the second was of me laughing, as though the world were wonderful, as though life were impervious to time. There were books about schizophrenia and medicine and neurobiology; old stereotaxic equipment; a Caithness paperweight I had gotten him on one of our trips to Scotland; a huge print of Van Gogh's *White Roses,* from the premiere of our Van Gogh film at the National Gallery of Art. I would keep the books and photographs and give the Van Gogh print to one of his friends.

What would I do with the stereotaxic equipment, which was part of a brain tissue transplantation system Richard and his colleagues had developed and patented to investigate possible treatments for Parkinson's disease? I pulled out the pieces, arranged the long brass screws in a circle, and obsessed. Should I throw them away? Richard had wanted them enough to keep them. Where would I put all of the pieces? I sat immobilized: Keep or throw away? Keep or throw away? Finally, I scooped them up like pick-up sticks, took them to the kitchen, and put them in a vase. They fell to the sides of the vase like metal flowers. Kept, but changed. I put the vase next to our wedding picture and smiled. He would like this, I thought.

The mail continued to jolt and on occasion offend. Bureaucracies are good at offending and, in this, the Medical Board of California yielded to none. "To whom it may concern," one of its letters began. "The Medical Board of California, Licensing Operations, has received information that Dr. Richard J. Wyatt may be deceased. If this is true, the Board sends its condolences to the doctor's family, friends, and associates. For Licensing Operations to make the necessary file changes, please provide us with a copy of the Certificate of Death." Dr. Wyatt would be missed by his California licensing board.

I went to England several months after Richard died. I was slated to give a talk and I wanted to get away from the world as it had become to me. Once there, I settled into the London Library and collected piles of books from the stacks—biographies of J. M. Barrie and Louis Armstrong, books about the stars—and immersed myself in work on my book about exuberance. I delved into the articles I had collected about the numbers of stars and galaxies in the universe, the numbers of grams of diamond stardust, and I read up on DNA base pairs in trumpet lilies and amoebae. I felt close to Richard, in the sense that I knew he would find the topics of interest, but I scarcely thought at all about the two of us. I realized that I was, for the first time, so absorbed in ideas and images that I had blotted out his absence and the pain of losing him. This infused a small amount of hope, in which I took great heart.

The reveling stopped at the library door. As soon as I walked outdoors I was hit by everything I had put out of my mind. What was I going to do? Where would I go? How could I bear London without Richard? Who would I talk to about stars and amoebae? For whom would I buy a tie? *I want my husband back.*

There it was again: the truth. *I want my husband back.*

A few days later in Warwick, at a European conference on suicide, I willed my way through my lecture and then sat in on some of the other clinical papers. I should have passed on this. All I remember is a recitation of the social risk factors for suicide: losing a spouse, living alone, not being married. It was clear. I was vulnerable not only in my brain, by disease, but in my heart. I knew this well enough; I didn't want to hear it. (Richard once summarized *Charlotte's Web* as "a wonderful story about a pig who is protected by a spider and how they take care of each other." We had been that way: protected. I didn't think about "risk factors" then.)

Later in the fall, on Richard's and my wedding anniversary, I slipped on my Roman ring and my ring of stars and, thus armed, went to Richard's grave. I tried to think about our wedding day but could not overcome his being now so cold and dead. Memory is pale next to life or death. I thought, The ground will freeze, the water in the vase in the ground will freeze, and then what will happen to Richard? I am alone, but he is so utterly alone. I cannot do anything for him now. There are so many things one thinks that one never thought to think about. I felt at sea, assailed, numb. I did not know what I thought or felt—everything was jumbled, in flux, and contrary.

I sat on the marble bench near his grave and read to myself poems by Thomas Hardy, Louis MacNeice, Edward Thomas, and Robert Bridges. The last verse of Bridges's "Poem," I read aloud, to Richard:

> *I will not let thee go.*
> *I hold thee by too many bands*
> *Thou sayest farewell, and lo!*
> *I have thee by the hands,*
> *And will not let thee go.*

And then I let him go, for a while.

That November, there was a new profusion of meteor showers. I tried to muster enthusiasm for it, but I could not. At midnight, I went outside to look for meteors but there was a full moon and I could see nothing. I went out again at five in the morning and this time saw several, but they held no wonder for me without Richard. Nothing could come close to our early morning in the park just a year earlier. I could not imagine that I would run away from shooting stars, but I did. I went indoors.

I knew that the Christmas season would be hard; I hoped only that it would not be too hard. There is so much memory wrapped up in Christmas, so much specificity. Richard liked white Christmas lights, I like colored ones; Richard preferred lights to blink, I do not. Each year we put up strands of nonblinking colored lights for me and strands of blinking white lights for him. It looked higgledy-piggledy, but lovely in its own odd way. On that first Christmas without Richard, I did not know what to do about Christmas lights, so I did nothing. I came home one evening to find that Silas Jones, who had worked for Richard and me for years and was, for both of us, a cross between close friend and father, had put up our strange strands of blinking and nonblinking lights. There we were, Richard and I together in spirit, lighting up the house and the yard. It was a warm moment in a cold season.

Trimming the tree was a melancholy affair. Ornament by ornament, I hung our memories on the tree. Gingerbread snowflakes, glass candy canes, an ugly clay parrot, handblown glass balls from London. In a small act of mourning, I did not put any tinsel on the tree. No one would notice, but it was of moment to me. Tinsel was a part of the excitement of childhood Christmases, its absence a bit of Lent.

I had to go to the store to buy more lights for the tree—I wished I could tell Richard this, but at least I could imagine his laugh. It was another good moment. That moment of imagined laughter could not last, of course. As I started to go out the door, I heard a crash, massive, and then tiny shatterings. The tree had fallen over, and several of our most sentiment-laden ornaments had shattered on the brick hearth. I am not superstitious, but I was, then, overcome with a dreadful foreboding. Darkness would come from darkness.

The following day, I took Richard's research assistant out to lunch and, in the midst of our conversation, told her that my Christmas tree had fallen down, how ominous it seemed, and that nothing like that had ever happened to me before. Her face turned pale. The previous evening, she said, her Christmas tree had fallen over—the first time that had ever happened to her—and three ornaments had been broken, including one Richard had given her ten years earlier. Perhaps, we decided, it was Richard, acting in ways best known to himself.

That afternoon, I laid branches cut from the bottom of the Christmas tree against the granite of Richard's gravestone. I listened to "Adeste Fidelis" and it pierced my heart, entered into it like a river that until that moment had been diverted. Richard slipped into my dreams that night. It started well. He and I were talking about going to a scientific meeting in Hawaii and I asked him, "Are you well enough to fly that far?"

He looked well, and said with surprise, "Yes, of course. Why do you ask?"

I felt a moment of unimaginable relief. Perhaps I had been wrong.

I said, "I think you are dead."

He held me close to comfort me, as he had so many times, and said, "It's Christmas, I know. I'm so sorry, sweetheart." And he left. It was so real, so much worse than not dreaming of him at all.

I could not face my own church on Christmas Eve. I had too many memories of being there with Richard, and I dreaded running into anyone I knew, so I went to the New York Avenue Presbyterian Church for their candlelight communion service. My mother had worshipped there as a young bride during World War II and listened to the great Peter Marshall; she spoke often of the sense of purpose and healing his sermons had brought to wartime Washington. Abraham Lincoln had sought solace in the church during the Civil War. It seemed a good place to go. I tried to sing the carols but couldn't and bolted from the church after the last one. It had snowed during the service and the trees and grounds of the city were white and first-snow beautiful. A bit of the magic of Christmas Eve came back. I thought, I will write "I LOVE YOU" in the snow on his grave on Christmas morning, and I felt my heart lighten. Driving home, my mood changed: the snow seemed an ominous thing on his grave, more constraining even than the earth. This was not the snow of childhood; it was the oppressive snow of having lived through too many winters.

I was never alone during the Christmas days, not for any consequential period of time. My friends and family and colleagues saw to that. Bob and Mary Jane Gallo, Jeff and Kathleen Schlom, Jeremy, my mother and brother and I went to 1789, a restaurant in Georgetown, shortly before Christmas, continuing Richard's and my tradition of going there on anniversaries and other special days, including the night we got married. In a tribute to friendship, and because Richard and I loved Wilson "Snowflake" Bentley's work, I gave everyone a Steuben crystal paperweight engraved with a snowflake. We christened ourselves "The Snowflake Club," in honor of our coming together as individuals, as snow crystals do, to form unique and stronger bonds as snowflakes. Each of us had our own history, shaped by our separate journeys, but we had hooked onto one another and come together, different and stronger. No matter the circumstances, great or grim, there was laughter, always; kindness, always; a generous giving of time, always. I trusted my life to each of them, as Richard had his.

That first Christmas after Richard's death, we, the newly christened Snowflake Club, listened to the carolers in front of the fire and lifted our glasses to Richard. The warmth and friendship helped me to overcome my missing of him to an extent I would not have thought possible. Only when the tables were quieter and the mood more reflective did I find myself near tears. I could feel Jeff watching me, his concern evident, so that even during the quiet moments it was not as grim as it could have been. It was the first night of winter.

Christmas morning, I flailed. I was as restless as I had been peaceful just a few days earlier. My grief was acute, stabbing. I had lost my mate; it was a primitive animal feeling. I was not depressed, I was simply overcome by waves of sadness. Such fizz and delight as I had had with life seemed long ago and bound to Richard. Richard is not here.

I want my husband back, I chanted yet again to myself. *I want my husband back.* It was a flat recitation that did not relieve the quiet terror. It didn't have a prayer.

Christmas night was less terrible than I thought it would be. For the first time I could remember, I was aware of *needing* Christmas. I needed the infusion of promise, of joy and remembrance, that came in the ancient rites and carols, the company of friends, and the lights in a dark season. There was life before Richard and there would be life after his death. I took this on faith and I almost believed it.

I turned a corner that Christmas after Richard died. Dread had outpaced the reality; a certain peace drifted into my world. Perhaps it was illusory. But the softness of the carols and the candlelight in the church darkness, beautiful and sad, stayed on for a while, after the season.

"A gentler feeling crept / Upon us," wrote Tennyson of the first Christmas after his friend Arthur Henry Hallam's death. "Surely rest is meet: / 'They rest,' we said, 'their sleep is sweet.' "

For a while, at least, there was some respite from the pain of missing Richard. I took roses out to his grave when I went, an act of defiance. The ice in the ground vase was uncrackable, so I splayed the flowers on the snow: scarlet against white and granite, blotches of life and fury.

The new year did not start well. Pumpkin was sick. She was sluggish and turned her nose aside when I offered her food. Even blueberries and Stilton cheese, her favorites, were left untouched. The veterinarian said that she had liver cancer and that it had spread; she would not live for long. He advised me to put her down. Silas and I talked about it and agreed that this was the kindest thing to do.

On Pumpkin's last day, I put on one of Richard's shirts so that a bit of him would be with her at the end, and then Silas and I held her while the vet gave her an intravenous tranquilizer and sodium pentothal. She just went, in peace, in every way different from the grotesque machinations attendant to Richard's death. Her long velvety ears lay out around her head, as they had always done. It was a quiet, dignified death.

The house felt hollowed out by Pumpkin's death. There were none of the distractions of funeral plans and visitors and family that had filled the house after Richard died. Now there was a new empty space beside me at night, a new quietness. There was no snuffling or snoring, no sounds of her walking around in circles on top of her bed. Six months earlier there had been two to say good-night to. Now there was no one. Pumpkin had been a part of my life with Richard for nearly fifteen years; an important tie to him was gone. She was gone. He was gone.

It was Silas who found the answer to some of his and my sadness about Pumpkin's death. He came into my study one afternoon with photographs and descriptions of basset hounds that were being fostered by a rescue program. He left the pictures on my desk and said, "I know it's too early. But it's something to think about." On his way out the door, he added, "There's one that has her feet up in the air. She looks kind of cute." I thanked him but told him it was far too early to be thinking about it. My heart was broken and past repair.

Silas is as intuitive as he is smart, and he knows me well. He had piqued my curiosity. I picked up the papers after he left; I didn't have a chance, as he well knew. The basset hound with her feet in the air was six years old and living in a foster home with nine other dogs. She looked like she had a certain pizzazz. We agreed it couldn't hurt to meet her.

A few days later, we drove out to Virginia to take a look. It was over before it began. Fifty-five pounds of basset came bounding over to me and licked my face, and that was that. I pulled out part of the money Richard had left in his basset fund and gave it to the rescue group. We named her Bubbles, for reasons obvious to anyone who met her. Pumpkin had been shy, content with life as it was, and timorous. Bubbles was effervescent and intrepid. They could not have been more different, which was a godsend.

Bubbles sat on my lap the entire way back to our house, nose sticking out of the window, comfortable with Silas and me, as if she had known us forever. When we arrived at the house, she ran directly into the garden room, looked around, leaped up onto the sofa, and walked along its top as if she were a cat. She stared briefly out into the garden, dropped gracefully down onto my new white rug, squatted daintily, and relieved herself. Bubbles had arrived.

It was good and necessary, having a new life in a house that had seen so much sickness and death.

La vie recommence—life starts again.

Not long after Bubbles joined the household, I drove down to North Carolina to give a talk at Duke University. The former president of the university and his wife had been good friends of Richard's and they had kindly extended their friendship to me. I spent the night at their house and they saw me off in the morning with a bag of homemade gingersnaps. When I returned home, I put the gingersnaps out of Bubbles's reach on the countertop. It was to turn out that nothing was out of Bubbles's reach; she turned chairs into stepladders, and her nose into a positioning device to move the chairs. Later that night, I went up to my bedroom and saw Bubbles asleep on the sofa with her nose resting on something. I thought for a moment that she had caught a squirrel, but it was the bag containing the gingersnaps. She had taken the bag from the kitchen counter and carried it upstairs, and was now guarding the cookies with her nose. For days she carried the bag of gingersnaps around with her. She never ate them.

Now and again, I would see in Bubbles the traces of days when she had lived in a household with children: an insistent paw raised to shake hands, a shameless grab for affection by rolling over on her back and kicking her feet. She displayed the vulnerability of having lost something that mattered. We were close that way. She had lost her family; I had lost Richard. We had each other now. It wasn't the same, but it was good. She was as gentle with my feelings as she had been with her bag of gingersnaps.

In the spring, I went to the American Psychiatric Association meetings in San Francisco and felt Richard's absence everywhere: at dinners with colleagues, where I was now just one, not half of a couple; at the scientific sessions, where I could scarcely concentrate well enough to follow the drift of the talks, and in trawling Drug Company Row. I went to my hotel room the first night of the meetings and wept. They meant nothing to me without Richard. There seemed little point to anything without Richard.

I had to force myself to go to the research poster sessions and listen to the young scientists present their data; they were enthusiastic and not yet wary of life. But forcing myself to go was a good thing. I was beginning to see that work was a saving grace, that listening to new ideas and promising clinical findings was important and sustaining. Richard had told me this on our last Valentine's Day: "Your work is important. It will help when you are missing me. It will draw us close." He was right. Work was a solid thing, a thing of intrinsic value. Writing and teaching take one through sadness, countervail it. Curiosity drives one forward; discovery confers life.

Richard was a romantic about science and ideas. I had loved him for this and it was a part of him that stayed close to me during the early, terrible times. Those things of the mind that we had shared were lasting things. They were things that had drawn us together when we first met and they were things we were talking about on our last day together. Richard took ideas seriously. He did not fritter away either his mind or time.

I thought of this side of Richard not long ago when I was at the University of Lund in Sweden to give a talk. It was early December and the ancient university town was lighted everywhere, with tiny white lights in the windows of houses and in the shops: so many bits of light and beauty against the dark. I wished, in a way that ached, that I could be with Richard in the town, share the experience of the town and its people and history with him, make love with him again, fall asleep in his arms. We both loved university towns, especially ones where learning and teaching had gone on for so many hundreds of years. We loved the feel of them; we loved the idea of them.

I had a memorable time in Lund with my Swedish colleagues, but I missed Richard. He would have noticed so many things; he would have loved Lund and its history of scientific thinking. He would have liked the seriousness with which the history of ideas was taken. One evening during dinner, I noticed that several of the Lund professors wore two gold rings instead of one. One was a wedding ring and the other, a colleague explained, was a gold ring given to them when they completed their doctoral examinations. I found this a singular thing, a vow to knowledge, as to God or a spouse, and it would have made its way into Richard's heart.

I had much work to get done after Richard died. I had to finish my book on exuberance and then, with a colleague, revise our fourteen-hundred-page medical text on bipolar disorders and recurrent depression. There was no choice but to work hard, and this was a blessing. I had slipped away from my profession during the years that Richard was ill. I wanted to return. I needed to return.

The initial year after Richard's death was the most difficult, the pain the most raw, the cobbling together of protective ways thin and fragmentary. This changed slowly. The first anniversary of Richard's death marked a small but symbolic juncture. My colleagues at an international conference on bipolar disorders presented me with an award for my work and asked me to make a few remarks. I said that I owed my life to the work of the hundreds of scientists and clinicians in the room, as did anyone who had bipolar illness. This was true, and it is something I felt deeply. Then I spoke about Richard, saying that he had died exactly a year earlier, that he had encouraged me to write about my illness. That he had supported me in every conceivable way as a husband, colleague, and friend. I could not go on. If I did, I knew I would fall apart.

My colleagues saw this, I think, and brought me back in the kindest possible way. They started to applaud, continued to applaud, and would not stop. Some whistled and cheered. It was a prolonged, extraordinary, and heartfelt response, one that not only brought a wave of warmth into my life when I needed it, but also reminded me that it is work that matters, work that is done in the context of love and life and death. I knew these things, of course, but my colleagues brought their importance back into my heart. All in the room were in the profession of healing; all worked to ameliorate suffering. It was one minute against a year, but I found renewal in that moment of generosity.

We put our faith in things great and small. We assign to them meaning they may actually have, or meaning that we need for them to have in order to carry on. I go to Richard's grave with flowers in my arms that I will to last, with orange tulips in one hand and a hammer to break the ice in another. Why and to what avail? That there is a vivid moment of color against the granite? It will not last.

Martin Luther, it is said, declared that even if the world were to end tomorrow, he still would plant his apple tree. Every Christmas, I go to Richard's grave and gather the evergreen boughs tight around the tulips and roses to warm them, to protect them for another hour. I find pleasure that there is beauty near Richard, even though it does not last. It is a small thing, but it matters. I do not want him to be forgotten, or to lie alone.

Mourning and Melancholia

I did not get depressed after Richard died. Nor did I go mad. I was distraught, but it was not the desperation of clinical depression. I was restless, but it was not the agitation of mania. My mind was not right, but it was not deranged. I was able to reason and to imagine that the future held better things for me than the present. I did not think of suicide. Yet Richard's death stirred up such a darkness in me that I was forced to examine those things depression and grief hold in common and those they do not. The differences were essential, the similarities confounding.

I did not, after Richard died, lose my sense of who I was as a person, or how to navigate the basics of life, as one does in depression. I lost a man who had been the most important person in my life and around whom my future spun. I lost many of my dreams, but not the ability to dream. The loss of Richard was devastating, but it was not deadly.

I knew depression to be unrelenting, invariable, impervious to event. I knew its pain to be undeviating.

Grief was different. It hit in waves, caught me unawares. It struck when I felt most alive, when I thought I had moved beyond its hold. *I am so much better dealing with his being gone,* I would say to myself, assured by some new pleasure in life. Then I would be flung far and cold by a wave of longing I could scarcely stand.

I learned to live in expectation of assault. From nowhere, a memory of Richard would compel me, like some recollected scent, into a region of my mind whose existence I had forgotten. Then I would coil to protect myself, huddle as prey against predator. *He cannot be gone,* I would rail against the gods, caught again in the presence of his absence. *He will not be back,* I would know after each new confrontation. It became clearer over time, less wavering. *He will not be back. He has been away too long.*

Grief taught through indirection. It was an unyielding teacher, shrewd and brutal. It attacked, soft and insidious at times, gale force at others, insistent that I see Richard from first one slant and then another—sometimes in fragments, at others full-on—until I could put him, and the two of us as we had been together, in the more distant place where all to do with him had to be. Memory and regret bypassed my rational mind and saw themselves straight into the festering places.

I fought hard against this, defiant. *If he cannot stay,* I would rail at Grief, *do not bring him back.* But grief teaches in its own way, and thoughts of Richard came and went in a manner not of my choosing. Grief, pre-Adamic and excellently evolved, knew how best to do what it had to do. Richard had to come and go, return and leave again, if he was to take leave in the way he must. He had to take leave in order that I might find a new place for him; in order that I might find a new way to be with him, in order for life to go on. Or so I found some peace in believing.

Grief, said C. S. Lewis, is like "a winding valley where any bend may reveal a totally new landscape." This is so. The lessons that come from grief come from its unexpected moves, from its shifting views of what has gone before and what is yet to come. Pain brought so often into one's consciousness cannot maintain the same capacity to wound. Grief conspires to ensure that it will in time wear itself out. Unlike depression, it acts to preserve the self. Depression is malignant, indiscriminately destructive. Grief may bear resemblance to depression, but it is a distant kinship.

Physically, I felt far better after Richard's death than I had during my bouts of depression. I slept restlessly but well enough, and when I did not, medication usually worked. My mind narrowed to a more insular universe. In an essential sense, I was alone. Grief, like depression, is a journey one must take largely unattended. I pulled in my dreams and kept company with the past. The future was set aside, put in abeyance. I had less energy, but enough to see me through. This is never so in depression. Weariness pervades the marrow when one is depressed; it is what renders despair intolerable. I bled out during my depressions. This was not so after Richard died. My heart broke, but it beat.

My mind knew that things were not right after Richard died; it knew that everything about me needed tending. Solitude allowed tending, and grief compelled solitude. Time alone in grief proved restorative. Time alone when depressed was dangerous. The thoughts I had of death after Richard's death were necessary and proportionate. They were of his death, not my own. When depressed, however, it was my own death I thought about and desired. It was my own death I sought out. In grief, death occasions the pain. In depression, death is the solution to the pain.

I was notably restless in the months after Richard died and, disturbed by this, I spoke to my psychiatrist, concerned that I might be getting ill again. He reassured me that such restlessness was an unavoidable and probably necessary part of grieving. In time, it became less distressing; it was never the perturbing agitation of mania. So, too, the sadness of grief was never so extreme as that of depression. It did not obliterate my reason. I was profoundly unhappy and distraught in the months after Richard died, but not hopeless. My mood, fixedly bleak during depression, was not so during grief. It was mutable and commonly rose in response to the presence of my family and friends. I was generally able to meet the demands of the world. I conserved my energy but was able to call upon it when I had to. Like a butterfly in the rain, I sought hiding places and kept my wings folded tight about me until I had no choice but to move. When I had to move, I did, albeit gingerly and not far. In time, the weather cleared. Even during the worst of my grief I had some sense that this would happen, that the weather would clear. I did not have this faith during the merciless months of depression.

My mind did not retain full clarity after Richard died. Far from it. But my confusion during grief was different from that which I had experienced when depressed. During both, I ruminated: my thoughts, repetitive and dark, churned over and over and made me doubt that I would ever create or love again. When I was depressed, however, each thought was not only dark but death-laden and punitive. No simple good came from the ruminations of melancholy.

Grief cut me more slack. Memories came unsought and disturbed my equanimity. Still, they carried with them an occasional sweetness, a periodic tincture of life. My thoughts did not dwell on the pointlessness of life; they dwelled, instead, on the pain of missing a life. Hope can find a place in a mind missing love. It cannot find a place in a mind taken over by depression. In grief, one feels the absence of *a* life, not life itself. In depression, it is otherwise: one cannot access the beat of life.

Grief, however, creates a strange sensitivity. The world is too intense to tolerate: a veil, a drink, another anesthetic is required to blot out the ache of what remains.

One sees too much and feels it, as Robert Lowell put it, "with one skin-layer missing."

After Richard died, I reflexively shied away from anything that might hit a minor key, sound a deeper note. I struggled to find ways to keep from being overwhelmed by what I saw and heard around me. I found solace at his grave, in part because of this disturbing sensitivity. I knew I would find quiet there. There was comfort in the old trees and in the stillness of the buried. I newly appreciated the colors of the earth; vibrant ones jangled my nerves, seemed garish and intrusive. For many months after Richard's death, I brought no primary colors into our house. I hung beige drapes and purchased dull linens and drab clothes. It was a beige time in my life, which I later took to calling my "antifrock" period. My new dresses were meant to conceal, to inhibit the responses of others. They were the opposite of summer frocks: they were anything but free and light.

The parts of me that froze when Richard died had to thaw slowly; otherwise, I would drown. Life had to return inchmeal; my heart could open up only small territories at a time. I turned by instinct to music to help with this, but it was not the solace I thought it would be. Only hymns, which quieted my nerves, brought predictable comfort. Schumann and Beethoven ripped my heart apart. Their music, ordinarily a source of immense pleasure, pierced me in a manner I found unbearable. The beauty was too human and yet unearthly: it was too intense, too direct an emotional hit. Schumann and

Beethoven awakened in me things best left alone. In the one completely irrational act of my grief, I gave away my entire classical musical collection. I did not want to have access to such pain.

I cloaked my senses in other ways. The first Christmas Eve after Richard's death I went to a Presbyterian church, not the Episcopal church to which I belong. In an immediate way, I did not want to run into people I knew or to remember times I had been there with Richard. More viscerally, I did not wish to risk a sudden flooding of memory at midnight. I did not want to come out of the church into a crisp night with bells ringing and the chance of snow. It would be a pure assault on the senses. Although confirmed as an Episcopalian, I had attended Presbyterian churches often over the years; for that first Christmas, I found the prospect of their services more gentling: less ancient in ritual, no kneelers and no kneeling, more congregational. Communion would be in the pews, not at the altar; wine would be in small cups, not in a silver chalice. The carols of Christmas Eve would be altogether more comforting than the Mass of Christmas morning. I would offset the intensity of the Anglo-Catholic liturgy with the sparer Scottish church tradition.

Yet my Presbyterian Christmas gave only the slightest of reprieves. When, toward the end of the service, the church was darkened and each of us sat with lighted candle and sang together "Silent Night," I cried. I cried, missing Richard. I cried because "Silent Night" was his favorite carol. I cried because there was really nothing I could do to keep his memory at bay.

"I miss him in the weeping of the rain," wrote Millay. "I miss him at the shrinking of the tide." Yes. But I miss him everywhere.

From the beginning, poetry consoled in a way that music could not. I read deeply, if fitfully, after Richard died. Such consolation was never possible for me during the times I was depressed. When depressed, I could not concentrate well enough to read; little made sense to me and the written word left me cold. When depressed, nothing could open my heart or give me courage. I was too dulled, too incapable of receiving life; I was dead in all but pulse. Only after depression took its leave could I turn to the experiences of those who had known deep despair or been mad—Robert Lowell, Byron: so many.

Grief, on the other hand, rendered me able to take solace from those who had written so well about loss and suffering. After Richard died, I turned instinctively to Tennyson's *In Memoriam,* which I had read when seventeen, recovering from my first siege of suicidal depression. I found it then, as I found it after Richard's death, to be an astonishing work: a passionate journey through suffering; a poem of great doubt and greater love. It is a poem that makes sense of the complexity and ferocity of grief, a poem of regret and renewal and letting go. Tennyson's grief is raw in *In Memoriam,* and in the nakedness of his pain is a peculiar, defining power.

Perturbation is elemental to Tennyson's elegy, and it was one of the things that first drew me in. He strews his poem with images of howling, blasting, lashing: rooks are "blown about the skies"; the sky is sown with "flying boughs." There is a "wild unrest that lives in woe." "Can calm despair and wild unrest / Be tenants of a single breast?" he asks. It is clear throughout that they can and are. Nature is portrayed as "careless of the single life," as "red in tooth and claw." Grief, for Tennyson, is a sickened and violent thing: "The blood creeps, and the nerves prick / And tingle; and the heart is sick." Time is "a maniac scattering dust, / And Life, a Fury slinging flame."

I found solace in Tennyson because I found his grapplings with grief so pained that I believed them. He wrote of the dreadful missing, the nights and seasons that pass unshared. He brought to his portrayal of grief lines of staggering beauty; he offered a solace that was not an easy solace. Each anniversary of death, each Christmas, each ringing in of the new year found in Tennyson a passing, a changing, an evolving apprehension.

There is no straight path in Tennyson's poem of grief. Understanding comes, only to dissipate; faith enters but to leave; and resignation to death is now and again incomplete. Yet death must be acceded to if it is to give way to life. This Tennyson makes clear in his great image of the wild, tolling bells:

Ring out, wild bells, to the wild sky,
The flying cloud, the frosty light:
The year is dying in the night;
Ring out, wild bells, and let him die.

Ring out the old, ring in the new,
Ring, happy bells, across the snow:
The year is going, let him go;
Ring out the false, ring in the true.

Ring out the grief that saps the mind . . .

Grief transforms the nature of how death is experienced. There is wisdom in the pain attached to grief; it is not irredeemable suffering. It is not suffering without an end: despair cannot indefinitely "live with April days, / Or sadness in the summer moons."

I found that in my old copy of *In Memoriam* I had bracketed lines toward the end of the poem. After Richard's death I wrote out these lines as an act of faith, a hope that I might grow into them. The years of grief, Tennyson had written, "Remade the blood and changed the frame, / And yet is love not less, but more":

Regret is dead, but love is more
Than in the summers that are flown,
For I myself with these have grown
To something greater than before.

Love is altered but remains. To read *In Memoriam* was to throw a summer wreath over an unclimbable fence in impassable weather. I could see life on the other side: the way over the fence would be hard, but the wreath gave me something to keep sight of, something toward which to move. Tennyson saw me through dark times. Words made a difference.

The capacity to be consoled is a consequential distinction between grief and depression. It is not that consolation is always possible during grief; it is not. It is, rather, that consolation is possible. We have, as individuals and societies, found ways to deal with grief.

Depression, less comprehensible than grief, does not elicit the same ritual kindness from others. Human nature keeps us at a greater distance from those who are depressed than from those who grieve. Grief does not alienate in the same way that depression does. It is different. Being a human thing, ancient and inevitable and given to all, grief draws together those who knew the dead, binds those who have cause to miss and mourn. It is in our human nature to extend tolerance and time toward those who are weary and confused while grieving: the loss is known, the emotions understood.

From the first death, the first grief. We know what our ancestors knew. They would, through their issue, lay down the rudiments of mourning: which bells to toll, why one veil and not another, how to pin a mourning brooch. Toward the depressed, society gives no such instruction, no such sanction. Grief and depression have always been part of the human condition, yet we treat them differently. The rituals of grief defend against alienation. Depression by its nature alienates. Grief alienates only when it is perceived by others to be too prolonged, too severe. That is, grief begins to alienate when it begins to bear likeness to depression.

I had known depression and mania since I was seventeen years old. What I experienced after Richard's death was grief, not depression or madness. In the early days after he died, when grief overwhelmed me and I could see no way out, I had hours of abject terror: What if my madness comes back? How will I keep my sanity with him not here? But these fears did not last for long.

Indeed, my close acquaintance with madness turned out to be a deft tutor for my passage through grief. It was strange that familiarity with despair and delusion would help me to deal with Richard's death: I had thought only to fear the return of sickness. But my struggles with manic-depressive illness had taught me more than I knew. I had a facility with extreme emotions and knew better than I would have liked how fast a mood can shift. I assumed suffering to be an integral part of life. My disease and my temperament, so beholden to each other, had taught me from the time I was young that contradictory and shifting moods were as real and meaningful as more settled, consistent ones. I had no expectation that calm was anything but a transient state. I knew, as well as I could know anything, that confusion and darkness inhabit lands next to light-filled and quiet ones.

I knew from experience that prior suffering buys no protection against future pain. (And nothing could prepare me for simply missing Richard.)

In a practical way, my long history of mania and depression had impressed upon me the symptoms to be most vigilant of; I knew to worry if I slept too little, got agitated, felt hopeless, thought of suicide. I was careful about this, perhaps overly so. Madness had prepared me for grief in other ways. It gave me an unsentimental gauge by which to test my sanity within my grief. It gave me a respect for the true terror that is at the core of madness: how inhuman it is; how far beyond grief it lies. When I knew grief, I knew in an odd way and for the first time how very sick I had been when mad. It was the difference between a confused mind and a delirious one, between agonal sadness and a knife across the carotid. It made me respect my mind more and look after it with a bit more tenderness.

The human nature of grief put the suffering of mania and suicidal depression in context: it was pain beyond describing and beyond solace. There was a sanity to my grief that kept the border strong between it and insanity. Mourning, as Freud made clear, is a natural part of life, not a pathological state. "Although grief involves grave departures from the normal attitude to life," he wrote, "it never occurs to us to regard it as a morbid condition and hand the mourner over to medical treatment. We rest assured that after a lapse of time it will be overcome." There are exceptions; some who grieve do need medical attention for depression, but most do not. Grief is not a disease; it is necessary.

Adversity proved good preparation for adversity. I believed, experience had taught me, that my desperate missing of Richard would pass. I believed that my restlessness would yield to ease, that night would find its way to day. I took it on faith, beneath my desperation and longing for Richard, that at some point, unannounced, a love for life would reemerge. I had been through so many cycles of darkness and light that I believed to my quick that nature would keep to her rhythms. If I survived madness, I said often to myself after Richard died, I can survive anything. I had found discipline and a harsh optimism from living on the edges of sanity. Richard had taught me not to lower my expectations of life in the presence of difficulty and not to squander love.

Many years earlier, after I had nearly died from my attempt to kill myself, I wrote out lines from Byron that I have kept since for courage: "Yet, see, he mastereth himself, and makes / His torture tributary to his will." Having been so ill in my mind did not allow me an easier or faster way through grief, but it did give me some way of seeing grief for what it is: a human thing.

"Blessing may break from stone," wrote George Mackay Brown. "Who knows how." Grief is such a stone. It gives much to the living, slows time that one might find a way to a different relationship with the dead. It fractures time to bring into awareness what is being mourned and why.

I remember an afternoon at the Natural History Museum in Washington, standing in front of a glass case filled with mummified owls. It seemed a violation of wild things to see such creatures stuffed and fakely perched. Yet had they not been dead and fixed, I could not have seen their wings and claws so clearly; I could not have appreciated the intricate beauty of their feathers and beaks. Had it not been for their deaths, I could not have seen what made them live. I would have preferred to have seen them fly or hunt or take a mouse to beak. But with them dead, I took in—with awe—their parts and proportions, saw in their stillness what made a snowy owl a snowy owl and not an Eastern screech. Death had something to give.

Grief, lashed as it is to death, instructs. It teaches that one must invent a way back to life. Grief forces intimacy with death; it preserves the salient past and puts into relief our mortal state. All die, says Ecclesiastes. All must die, it is written in the first statute of the Magna Carta. All die, teaches Grief.

"Sometimes I think that the search for suffering and the remembrance of suffering are the only means we have to put ourselves in touch with the whole human condition," wrote Graham Greene. Grief is at the heart of the human condition. Much is lost with death, but not everything. Life is not let loose of lightly, nor is love. There is a grace in death. There is life.

Fugitive Dyes

In the Shenandoah Valley, they say that spring climbs the mountains a hundred feet a day. Like grief, the spring will catch you unawares. You have become used to winter; it has in its own way served you well. The new season is not what you know. It is fresh and it comes from death.

Even as Richard was newly dead, I knew there was inside of me a reservoir of life. There was so much laughter the night he died—my friends and family and I laughed hard and well that evening—and where there is laughter, however dark, there is life. I knew there was life because I saw it in the faces of my friends and I felt it in the warmth of my family. Life seemed possible to me then, in the kindness of people I loved; later I knew it in the kindness of strangers who reached out with a word or a touch.

A few days after Richard died, I went to a small dinner party at the residence of the British ambassador. Jim Watson was being knighted for his codiscovery of the structure of DNA, an occasion Richard and I had hoped to share. Now I drove there alone; had it not been for my long friendship with Jim, and my inexpressible gratitude to him for his help during Richard's illness, I would have stayed at home. As I turned from Massachusetts Avenue onto the embassy's grounds, I suddenly remembered what Richard had said to me after Jim called to invite us to the investiture.

"I hope I live long enough to make it." Richard laughed. "I would give anything to see Watson on his knees."

I laughed out loud, remembering this. Richard was in the car with me for a moment and, where Richard was, where I laughed because of the memory of him, there was life.

It was a soft June evening and the gardens were spilling over with roses. Richard would have loved everything about the occasion: the gentleness of the Washington summer night, the company of friends, the ambassador's evocation of the high magic days of two young scientists doing shatteringly important work in postwar Cambridge, and the elegant celebration of one of the great discoveries in science. The evening was all these things, but what opened up a sliver of my heart to life again was that every person on the British Embassy staff, from the attendant who parked my car, to the person who checked off my name at the table in the entry hall, to the ambassador and his wife, said, "I am so sorry, Madam, for the loss of your husband." It was a small thing, but it was intensely important to me. It was an extension of civility in the face of death; it was an acknowledgment of my grief. The rituals of queen and government went on, the conversations of science went on, human kindness went on. I went on.

My heart thawed slowly back into life. In time, things that had overwhelmed me in the early months after Richard died came back and now gave pleasure again. I thought one evening to see if I could listen to music without the pain it earlier had caused me. I put on *Orfeo* and it broke my heart, but it was a heartbreak that promised life. The music did not rip open my heart any wider than it could at the same time heal.

Each day, each week, I pushed further, thinking to see how much life I could let back in before having to dart to the safety of sleep or a restless walk. When at last I reached out to Schumann and Beethoven, I listened to them with deep pleasure; there was no pain. I knew their beauty differently for having had to put them aside: I loved them more because of the vulnerability they had opened up in me.

Coming again to life was a hard but good thing. Life was in front of me now; the glove had been thrown down. I could not back away from the world: my temperament and my curiosity about what lay ahead made certain of this. Life had to be taken up again; the ribbons, woven flat against the maypole, had to be unwound. The future, inevitably, had become more inviting than the past. I was uneasy with grief, impatient with my life. I had spent too long in the company of illness and death. I did not want to do this any longer.

Sentiment and reminiscence, necessary at the beginning of grief, were now in active competition with life. Blood had to get to tissue: I wanted to yank back the tedious beige curtains I had hung. Mourning had forced me to reckon with death, but imagining forward was life. If I was to take seriously Richard's life and death, and my own, I would have to turn dead-on toward life. I had no interest in sewing my own shroud. Time was indeed a healing thing.

Richard had often talked about his experiences with Hodgkin's disease with other patients who suffered from it, hoping to give them encouragement and practical advice. One woman, with whom he had spoken many times, eventually died of her disease. Richard wrote to her brother about time and grief: "I have wondered about time's ability to heal," he wrote. "To me, it is a moving away or growing around the wound, nothing ever filling the void; new things diverting attention. The pain does not diminish, but the dilution by life's momentum makes the amount of time thinking about it and the suffering decrease." He was right. Life's momentum is a powerful thing.

In the immediate weeks and months after Richard died, I had turned to poetry and other literature for solace. Now I turned to them to see how to make my way back to life. I took down Tennyson again, and Douglas Dunn's *Elegies.* I reread Graham Greene's *The End of the Affair* and Lewis Grassic Gibbon's *Sunset Song.* I went back to my old and much margin-noted copy of William Bradford's *Of Plymouth Plantation,* to put in mind the role of will in overcoming adversity, and to hold up before me the absurdly easy physical dimensions of my life. I copied out great chunks of Edward Thomas and Louis MacNeice and Thomas Hardy, and taped to my mirror the final lines of Robert Frost's "Reluctance."

"The heart is still aching to seek," he had written. "But the feet question 'Whither?' ":

Ah, when to the heart of man
Was it ever less than a treason
To go with the drift of things,
To yield with a grace to reason,
And bow and accept the end
Of a love or a season?

I had no choice but to bow to a kind of end to love, but it *was* a treason to go with the drift of things. No one could fight this drift but me. Just do it, I said to myself. Just do it. There was comfort in looking backward, but it was beginning to take the air from the room. "The shadow kills the growth," wrote Ben Jonson. The shadow of Richard's death was long.

Memories of Richard continued to drift in and out of my mind as it reknit. Sometimes they jarred, at other times they added a sweet moment of pleasure to my days. My dreams of him changed. Lost was the pervasive feeling that he would come to me only to leave. My dreams were kinder now. In one, I remember, I was in a meadow and saw a man gasping for breath, poisoned by chlorine gas.

I said to him, "Wait, my husband is a doctor. He will be here soon."

My heart dropped as I remembered: He will not be here soon; he is dead. The old terror hit then, but Richard appeared and smiled and I felt his warmth come into me. Life was right again. I woke up easy in my mind for it was the first time in my dreaming of him that he had not left.

Another day, working on my book about exuberance, I reached for my research folder containing my interviews and notes about Joyce Poole, a biologist who studies elephants in Kenya. Tucked into the file, I found an e-mail Richard had sent to her. "Kay is away today," he had written, "but has been not very patiently awaiting your response. Not being patient is a fairly common trait, I think, among exuberant people. Which she is. I will read her your response later today. I think it is just what she is looking for." He then went on to offer his own entirely unsolicited observations about exuberance and creativity. How totally Richard. It was as if he had gently parachuted down into a thicket of someone else's ideas and made himself at home.

Mark Twain told a friend that after his wife died memories of her would come as an occasional grace note, "memories of little intimate happenings of long ago that drop like stars into the silence." Richard kept dropping stars my way. (Stars. I read not long ago that astronomers discovered streams of ancient stars streaking past the Milky Way at a million miles an hour. It is an image I long to share with Richard. Will I always think of him when I think of stars? Will I ever think of another man?)

I kept close to me memories of Richard that I particularly loved. Some refused to leave; others I wanted with me because they were him and us and I loved calling them up when in a blue mood or when simply missing him: our Los Angeles day of dire wolf skulls and aspens and rainbow trout; the vision of roses and lilacs floating in our bath in Rome; a gold ring dipped in the Trevi Fountain. Other things of Richard I kept but changed. I found it rending to look at the moonstone and aquamarine bracelet he had designed for me in California, so I took it to a jeweler and had it reconfigured into a necklace: the same elements together in a different way.

A *New York Times* reporter wrote about a small octopus that carried a brown bottle wherever it went: "When a human leaves it a much grander bottle, large and clear with a multimasted sailing ship inside, the octopus investigates the gift, considers for a moment, then picks up its beloved brown bottle and goes on its way." I understood this small octopus perfectly. I did not want a new, multimasted sailing ship; I wanted what I had had and loved.

There continued to be times of terrible missing. I opened the *Archives of General Psychiatry* one day and saw Richard listed as an author on a paper about schizophrenia. My heart raced. I have to show this to him, I thought. If his name is on the article he must still be alive. Then I saw the superscript next to his name and traced it to the footnote at the bottom of the page. "Deceased," it read. Yes, of course. Deceased. Later that night I woke up, aware that I had forgotten to take my lithium. Richard would have asked if I had taken it, I thought. Richard is dead, I snapped to myself. Enough. Get over it.

Over time, solace more than pain came from my memories of Richard. Thoughts of him were sweeter, less often jagged, stabbing things. There is a time limit to grief, I began to understand. Grief will end. I am alive. I love Richard, but I love life as well. Grief was beginning to wear out its welcome.

"But though this had been a day and night of much trouble," wrote William Bradford, "yet God gave them a morning of comfort and refreshing." Life was on the other side of grief, morning on the far side of a hard night.

Grief had changed the landscape of what had been our common life and settled happiness. Everything we had been together had been thrown into disarray. Revelation's dragon had swept its tail round the heavens, flinging stars to Earth and rearranging the sky: all that mattered was differently ordered from what I had known. Richard had created a quiet place for me; our life was lived at a gentler pace than I had known in my earlier, hurtling world. He had been a constant in an inconstant universe. Death had in some ways preserved him. It was I who must change, our relationship that must change. I did not wish to lose Richard but I would, unless our relationship was open to the possibilities of life.

I made a list of things to do. I would take up squash again; try to get through *Pride and Prejudice* again; learn more substantively about bits of nature I loved, but knew only in a dilettante way: plum blossoms, spotted quolls, spectacled bears. The list of natural phenomena I wished to better understand was long, but I would start with these. I would study neurology in a more systematic manner; visit Saint Petersburg and the Orkney Islands; see if I could arrange a trip to observe the elephants in Kenya's Amboseli National Park. I would begin again my weekly lunches at the National Gallery of Art and take up again my walks to the National Zoo. It seemed like a manageable list. I taped it to my mirror next to the excerpt from the Frost poem.

I set out to understand Richard better. The neurosurgeon Harvey Cushing stressed that what one accomplishes in one's work does not die. I believe this, so I decided to read Richard's scientific papers, first to last, in order to have a deeper understanding of his scientific work. This was to send myself on a fool's journey; he had written more than eight hundred papers, many of them highly technical. I read as best I could as many of them as possible. I thought I knew the range of his intellectual interests but I did not, and I felt closer to him for having followed where his brain had taken him during his scientific life.

I learned about him in other ways. Richard loved to listen to audiobooks and liked to have me read aloud to him. Reading had come easily to me; I had not known books in his way. I thought I would try to hear books as he had heard them. On Christmas day, three years after his death, I took Isak Dinesen's *Out of Africa* to his grave; he had loved listening to her book and had encouraged me to do the same. I had pleaded lack of time and never did it. Now I sat on the bench near his grave and began to read aloud: "I had a farm in Africa, at the foot of the Ngong Hills," I began. And then I read on and on, caught up in the beauty and cadence of her words, until I had to stop.

Dinesen wrote of Africa, but as I looked around me, I thought, This is true of where I am now: "You woke up in the morning and thought: Here I am, where I ought to be." Reading at Richard's grave on Christmas morning, I thought: I am where I ought to be. This city is my home. Washington is the city of my childhood and the better part of my adolescence, it is where Richard and I met and where we fell in love, it is where we lived and worked together. Washington is where he lies, and it is where we will lie together until the world ends, or until a parish ordinance mandates the resettling of bones.

But not yet.

I was caught that Christmas morning between death and life, but I was inclined, unstoppably, into life. I had a covenant with Richard, but I had one with the future as well. "Tonight I saw the stars trapped underneath the water," wrote Douglas Dunn. "I signed the simple covenant we keep with love. / One hand held out an apple while the other held / Earth from a kirkyard where the dead remember me."

I acted on my covenant with love in private and public ways. I planted a weeping cherry tree at Richard's grave and watched it grow graceful and gentle, complexly branched. I completed at last a needlepoint tapestry I had been working on for ten years, a wreath of moss roses against a background of navy blue. I had started it in London and given it to Richard on our wedding night. We lay together that night and listened to Paul Robeson sing the seventeenth-century words of Ben Jonson. The rosy wreath in my needlepoint was my marriage gift:

I sent thee, late, a rosy wreath,
Not so much honouring thee,
As giving it a hope, that there
It could not withered be.
But thou thereon did'st only breathe,
And sent'st it back to me:
Since when it grows, and smells, I swear,
Not of itself, but thee.

It was the final verse of a poem about the transcendent nature of love and about renewal; it said all I felt for Richard. The tapestry had been nearly finished by our wedding night, but not quite: as was my wont, my enthusiasm had exceeded my accomplishment. Ten years later, too late for Richard to see, I took up my needlepoint again. It galled me that I had been so blasé with time, that I had left the wreath unfinished. I do not think Richard would have cared, but I did. I regretted so many things left undone.

More recently, I donated in Richard's memory a collection of photographs to the Johns Hopkins Hospital. They are images of artist Anna Schuleit's floral tribute to patients institutionalized at Harvard's Massachusetts Mental Health Center, where Richard did his residency. Schuleit had observed what those who work in psychiatric hospitals know all too well: patients on psychiatric wards, unlike those on medical and surgical ones, seldom receive flowers from their visitors. Moved by this, she created a remarkable installation, *Bloom.* She filled the hospital with twenty-eight thousand potted flowers and arranged them by color on each of the four floors. Live sod—forty-nine hundred square feet of it—was laid out wall-to-wall in the basement. She planted two thousand pots of African violets, blue pansies, ferns, and heathers in the hallways, offices, and patient rooms. Fifteen thousand orange tulips were trucked to Boston to add color and to pay respect to the hospital and to those who had lived and been treated there. Hundreds of these tulips were later replanted on the unmarked graves of patients at a state asylum.

Richard, who trained at the Mass Mental in the early days of psychopharmacology, had gotten into frequent and heated arguments with his psychoanalytically trained clinical supervisors there. He found it inexplicable to have to justify using medications in patients with psychotic illnesses such as schizophrenia and mania. The experience made a deep impression upon him and taught him to question received wisdom in psychiatry. It also made him even more determined to find new ways to treat the severe mental illnesses.

I thought that giving these photographs to Hopkins, a place whose scientific and clinical traditions he admired and was beholden to, would create a symmetry of sorts. The photographs would also, perhaps, call to mind the life of a doctor and scientist who, like so many of his colleagues, had done what he could to alleviate the suffering of those with mental illness.

George MacKay Brown spoke about the preservation

of things. He had, he said, a "deep-rooted belief that what has once existed can never die: not even the frailest things, spindrift or clover-scent or glitter of star on a wet stone." Words and thoughts and actions preserve. They preserve differently than one might choose, but they do preserve.

Grief had taught, if nothing else, that to move forward I would have to imagine a life without Richard. The place I kept for him could not be one that continued to keep the future on ice. Reconstituting Richard and our relationship would mean reconstituting myself. I had no counsel for this but experience and the imagination of everyday life. I had often said to my patients who were struggling in the wake of mania or suicidal despair: We are each an island. It is your task to bring to your own island what you need to live long and well: love, beauty, diversion, friends; work that sustains; a meaningful life. Look at Maui, I would say: everything was brought in by man, insect, bird, or wind. It is your life; it is short. Treat your island with regard. Do not let it go to weed; do not give it over to anyone else. Understand the possibilities. Know the dangers. Keep away the ungenerous and the unkind.

Inventing places had always been what I did best. As a child, I had constructed worlds around me to contain my bubbling enthusiasms, to keep my dreams out of harm's way and to set them in order. When very young, I had loved *Katy No-Pocket*, the story of a mother kangaroo who was born without a pouch. Her life changed in every way when a construction worker gave her a carpenter's apron so that she could carry not only her own baby, but the babies of the other animals as well. I was captivated by the idea of having masses of pockets of different shapes and sizes that could hold my ideas and projects. In my mind's eye, I filled them with notebooks and colored pencils, my kaleidoscope and a magnifying glass, books and vials and my rapidly expanding family of pet mice.

In the third grade, I took this carpenter's apron inward. I imagined a life for my mind inside the shell of a many-roomed turtle. I hung clouds on door hooks, and filled an alcove with bins of stars. There was a separate area for my microscope, books, and experiments, and a dirt room for my lizards and mice. In the center, I constructed an open aviary for my songbirds, my parrot, and my great horned owl. Sometimes, during class, I would retreat into my shell and take a cloud down from its hook, blow into it, and send it on its way. Now and again, I would pick a star from its bin and sketch it, spin it round, or cradle it in my hands. At other times, I would dress up the mice in tiny cowgirl outfits.

The turtle was a reassuring, if unlikely, fiction. I was by nature an extrovert, quick-moving and talkative; configuring myself as a turtle could scarcely have been more improbable. Yet wandering around inside my shell allowed me to escape dull teaching, create order from clutter, and give shape to my hopelessly scattered thoughts and daydreams. My imagination was a good friend to me.

Later, I would create mental sanctuaries to help me contend with madness and despair. It was part of a lifelong struggle to sort through experience and to still my ways. Richard had been good for me in this regard; he had kept my mind from pelting off in all directions. He had tamped it down in his quiet way and kept its cascades within the riverbanks. I imagined less when he was alive; I did not need my islands of conjured places and imposed rhythms. But when he died, I sought again the kind of construing that would help me with my grief. The future was a place like any other; it could be imagined.

I was aided in my resolution to move forward in my life by the book I was writing about exuberance. While Richard was alive it had given me purpose and both of us heart. I liked the people whose passionate lives I was studying, and Richard had liked, each morning, for me to read to him what I had written. It was a pleasure jointly held. After he died, the idea of writing a book about joy seemed absurd to me. Exuberance seemed ridiculous, vapid, and irrelevant. I could not imagine why I had found the topic important. Exuberant by nature, I now found it hard to enter into the lives of my subjects, harder still to write about them. I had been weaving a tale for Richard's mornings and nights, brewing a physic to keep death away. It hadn't worked. He was dead. It seemed another of my chagrining enthusiasms.

Inevitably, as grief let up and I took to life again, writing about joy seemed a more comprehensible, and indeed a quite wonderful, thing to do. I had written, before Richard died, about love and exuberance and why they are essential to who we are as a species. Now I had to know how to end the book, for I knew somehow that I would find in the ending what Richard had given to me. I knew this with certainty, but it was a certainty based on faith, not reason.

The final chapter, which was to focus on discovery and the restless optimism of the American pioneers, became a treatise on imagination and the resilience of human nature. This chapter, I said to myself, will be for Richard. This will be what Richard brought back to me, and it is what I will give to him. Everything in this chapter, I knew, would be for Richard, and from that point on I had little difficulty in finishing the book.

I wrote, in the final chapter, about the resilience of the men and women who had sailed on the *Mayflower* in 1620 with only hope and will and the capacity to imagine the future. They had exerted their will and engaged their capacity to imagine against high seas and famine and disease; they survived. I wrote about Willa Cather's *O Pioneers!* and what she had said about the mind of the pioneer that "should be able to enjoy the idea of things more than the things themselves." I described Vachel

Lindsay's expansive, wandering Johnny Appleseed, who carried life into the frontier and into the future: "In that pack on his back, / In that talisman sack. . . . / Seeds and tree-souls, precious things, / Feathered with microscopic wings." And I recounted Ole Rölvaag's great saga of the Dakota plains, about the pioneer Per Hansa, in whom "there dwelt high summer" and "a divine restlessness," a man of surpassing imagination, who "strode forward with outstretched arms toward the wonders of the future." Pioneers, Rölvaag wrote, were those who had thrown themselves "blindly into the Impossible, and accomplished the Unbelievable."

I wrote of the expansive, roaming spirits of Whitman and Lindbergh and others who had reached for territories beyond. Finally, and most to my heart, I wrote of the life that comes from death: of the emergence of the great fields of flowers on the Somme battlefield where death had been all-dominant and not a tree was left alive; of Peter Ackroyd's description of beauty and life even in the wake of the German bombings of London during World War II. The streets, he wrote, bloomed with ragwort, lilies of the valley, and white and mauve lilac. There was life, even in the midst of devastation.

I found my way back into life through my writing, as Richard had told me I would, and in the end I found it easier than I thought it would be. I was writing for Richard and about him; I was writing about his enthusiasm for discovery, and the pleasure his mind took in new ideas and new places. I was writing about the life he had given back to me in the wake of my manias and depressions, about love and how it returns in its own way, in its own time. I was writing about the mystery of joy and the joy of love. Richard was dead, but love and ideas were not. Richard had taught me a saving amount and we had, in our common life, headed instinctively to the fields beyond. We always had looked yonder.

The mind imagines, even as it knows that its imaginings are fleeting things. When I was in Scotland two years ago, on my yearly lectureship at the University of St. Andrews, I opened the curtains in my room to see the Old Course and the town covered in snow. The North Sea was white, and one had to know that it was there in order to imagine it. Everywhere I looked it was breathtakingly beautiful. I went to chapel with a friend, and by chapel's end a large snowman, with stone eyes and a university scarf around its neck, had appeared in the college quadrangle. By teatime, snowmen of all sizes and in all manner of neckwear dotted the Old Course, the college gardens, and the gardens of the town. In so many places, the students and the townspeople had built snowy defiances of time, small tributes to imagination and impermanence.

The next morning, the grass was poking up through the snow, but three snowmen still stood on the Old Course. Within the hour, the grounds crew was chopping them up and the magic of the day before was gone.

It didn't matter. The creators of the snowmen had placed their joy in the creating, fully knowing the transience of their creations. The life of a snowman was short, its cold sands would soon be run, but the very fact that it was ephemeral made its existence a glorious thing. "The hands which give are taking," wrote the Scottish poet William Soutar. "And the hands which take bestow: / Always the bough is breaking / Heavy with fruit or snow."

It is in our nature to want to hold on to love; it is grief's blessing that we come to know that there are limits to our ability to do so. To hold on to love, I had to find a way to capture and transform it. The only way I knew to do this was to write a book, this book, about Richard. It would be about love and what love had brought, about death and what death had taken. I would write that love continues, and that grief teaches.

I returned to Big Sur, sat up against the cushions in the window seat in my room overlooking the rocks and the sea, and picked up the fountain pen Richard had given me years earlier to write *An Unquiet Mind*. Richard had said then, Write from your heart, and I had. I would write again from my heart, but this time I would write alone.

I sat for a long time, looking out on the rocks of the

Big Sur, which I had known long before I had known Richard. I started to write. I wrote about the durability of love and hope, about a man I had been with for nearly twenty years, a man who had been my husband, colleague, and friend. I wrote about fearlessness and grace and the power of love. I poured my heart into my writing, and when I walked on the beach at Big Sur Richard was with me there. He was with me in the quietening of my mind. Richard was with me in Big Sur, and he would be with me when I left Big Sur. It would not be the journey we had reckoned on, but it was what we had. We both were inclined to look yonder.

Acknowledgments

I owe much to the kindness of others. My greatest debt is to my family and friends; within that group, I am particularly indebted to "The Snowflake Club": Jeremy Waletzky, Robert and Mary Jane Gallo, Jeffrey and Kathleen Schlom, Silas Jones, and my brother, Dean Jamison. All have been unbelievably kind to me, as they were to Richard before he died. I once tried to thank them for everything they had done but could not find the words. Instead, I borrowed Byron's tribute to his friend John Hobhouse: "To one[s], whom I have known long, and accompanied far, whom I have found wakeful over my sickness and kind in my sorrow, glad in my prosperity and firm in my adversity, true in counsel and trusty in peril—to friend[s] often tried and never found wanting." I have been blessed, as Richard was, by these friends, whom we never found wanting. I will always owe a deep-felt debt to Thomas O'Connor, as well, who helped me to shape the beginning of this book, and supported me throughout my writing of it.

I am particularly grateful for the friendship and support of Raymond De Paulo, M.D., and Adam Kaplin, M.D., Ph.D, colleagues in the Johns Hopkins Department of Psychiatry, and to Hopkins surgeon Jacek Mostwin, M.D., D.Phil., whose discussions with me about medicine, literature, and life I value more than I can say.

I would like to thank others who provided friendship and/or who read earlier versions of this book and made helpful suggestions: Joanne Althoff, Robert Barnett, Samuel Barondes, Larry Blossom, Keith and Brenda Brodie, James Campen and Phyllis Ewen, Robert and Alice Crawford, Jacqueline Davies, Douglas Dunn, Robert and Kay Faguet, Christina and Antonello Fanna, Stephen Fried and Diane Ayres, Charles and Peggy Gosnell, Donald Graham, William Graham, Ara Guzelimian, John Harper, Charles and Gwenda Hyman, Stuart Kenworthy, Helen Kindle, Athanasios Koukopoulos, Wendy Lesser, Heidi Jamison, Marshall, Linda, Danica, and Kelda Jamison, Walter Johnson, Phillip Mallett, Andreas Marneros, Paul McHugh, Christopher Mead, Sallie Mink, Alain Moreau, John Julius Norwich, Clarke and Wendy Oler, Robert and Elaine Packwood, Regina Pally and James Korb, James Potash, Harriet Potik, David and JoAnn Reiss, Norman Rosenthal, Jerilyn Ross and Ronald Cohen, Barbara Schweizer, Sabrina Serrantino, Richard and Jill Sideman, Karen Swartz, Bety and Carlos Tramontana, Per

Vestergaard, Jim and Liz Watson, Peter Whybrow, and Kin Bing Wu. Joanne Leslie, who is like a sister to me, was close to Richard as well. Her participation in the rites of Richard's burial was particularly meaningful to our family.

Richard received excellent medical care from his internists in Washington, Drs. David Patterson and Bryan Arling; Dr. Kenneth Baughman, his cardiologist at Johns Hopkins (now at Harvard); and Drs. Richard Ambinder and David Ettinger, his oncologists at Johns Hopkins. His medical and nursing care at Hopkins was uniformly excellent, which made a difficult situation less difficult. Dr. James Watson was kind enough to get us in touch with the late Dr. Judah Folkman at Harvard, whose generosity with his time and whose treatment protocol almost certainly extended Richard's life by many months.

This book would not have been possible without the incomparable help of William Collins and Ioline Henter. Most particularly, I could not have written this book or managed my life without the help and friendship of Silas Jones. I am grateful for financial support from the Dalio Family Foundation, the Dana Foundation, and the John D. and Catherine T. MacArthur Foundation.

I, like many nonfiction writers, have been concerned about the damage done to the credibility of autobiographical writing by those who have written fraudulently about their lives. I have provided my editor at Knopf with extensive documentation for what I have written in *Nothing Was the Same.* This documentation includes copies of Richard's letters to me and mine to him, which are quoted from in this book; relevant contemporaneous accounts of events portrayed, as well as excerpts from journals and letters, correspondence from colleagues, friends, and the public; copies of public records; and copies of Richard's lectures and writings that are quoted in the book. In deference to privacy, I chose not to write about Richard's former wife and his children.

Carol Janeway, my editor at Knopf, has been a close friend and an excellent editor; she was a good friend to Richard as well. I am very appreciative of the help of David Nee, also at Knopf, and that of my copyeditor, Sibylle Kazeroid.

My mother, Dell Jamison, died before I finished writing this book. She believed that the most important thing in life is not the cards that one is dealt, but how one plays them. She was, by far, the highest card I was dealt.

Permissions Acknowledgments

Grateful acknowledgment is made to the following for permission to reprint previously published material:

Faber and Faber Ltd.: Excerpt from "The Apple Tree" from *New Selected Poems* by Douglas Dunn. Reprinted by permission of Faber and Faber Ltd.

Henry Holt and Company, LLC and The Random House Group Ltd.: Excerpt from "Reluctance" from *The Poetry of Robert Frost,* edited by Edward Connery Lathem, copyright © 1934, 1969 by Henry Holt and Company. Copyright © 1962 by Robert Frost. Reprinted by permission of Henry Holt and Company, LLC and The Random House Group Ltd.

Iain Antony Macleod and The Joseph Macleod Estate: Excerpt from "Love Song" by Joseph Macleod (Adam Drinan) (*Poetry Scotland,* 1949). Reprinted by permission of Iain Antony Macleod and The Joseph Macleod Estate.

National Library of Scotland: Excerpt from "Song" by William Soutar. Reprinted by permission of the Trustees of the National Library of Scotland.

A Note About the Author

KAY REDFIELD JAMISON is Professor of Psychiatry at the Johns Hopkins University School of Medicine. She is codirector of the Johns Hopkins Mood Disorders Center and a member of the governing board of the national Network of Depression Centers. Dr. Jamison is also Honorary Professor of English at the University of St. Andrews in Scotland. She is the author of the national best sellers *An Unquiet Mind* and *Night Falls Fast,* as well as of *Touched with Fire* and *Exuberance.* She is the coauthor of the standard medical text on bipolar illness, *Manic-Depressive Illness: Bipolar Disorders and Recurrent Depression,* and author or coauthor of more than a hundred scientific papers about mood disorders, creativity, and psychopharmacology. Dr. Jamison is the recipient of numerous national and international scientific awards, as well as a John D. and Catherine T. MacArthur Fellowship.

A Note on the Type

The text of this book was set in Centaur, the only typeface designed by Bruce Rogers (1870–1957), the well-known American book designer. A celebrated penman, Rogers based his design on the roman face cut by Nicolas Jenson in 1470 for his Eusebius. Jenson's roman surpassed all of its forerunners and even today, in modern recuttings, remains one of the most popular and attractive of all typefaces. The italic used to accompany Centaur is Arrighi, designed by another American, Frederic Warde, and based on the chancery face used by Lodovico degli Arrighi in 1524.

Composed by North Market Street Graphics, Lancaster, Pennsylvania

Printed and bound by RR Donnelley, Harrisonburg, Virginia

Designed by Maggie Hinders

34 Beaufort Gardens
London SW3
27 November 1985

Dearest Richard,

In the midst of seemingly unbelievable happiness with you, London, life I find myself unsure and dark and full of black thoughts and feelings. It came on as I suppose it always does with a sense of tiredness then the long deep black clouds and finally just despair and Why again? What's the point one's born just to die, feeling good is unreal and only to mock and haunt me when ill.

And for a brief while I thought I have Richard and if he were here or I were there he would hold and love me and make me a cup of tea give me a pill to let me sleep through the hard rough part.

There are moments when you provide a minute of sweetness and belief and then the blackness comes again. I think I shall be done for one of these times it just seems to accumulate sorrow and grief somewhere inside which only wait until the next time to come out again and remind me how always tides go out once in.

This is a ridiculously self indulgent letter though probably much of what I believe to be so. What isn't here is the depths of my love for you though it must be obvious, as the dark always reflects the light.

Kay